College Writing Models

With Workbook, Reader, and *MLA Handbook* Cross-references

Daniel V. Runyon, Ph.D.

Library of Congress Cataloging-in-Publication Data

Runyon, Daniel V.
College Writing Models
Includes bibliography
ISBN: 978-1-878559-09-8

Cover Design: Lisa Kaatz
Cover Photograph: "Aran Islands" by Lisa Kaatz
Publisher: Saltbox Press, Spring Arbor, MI

Daniel V. Runyon
167 Burr Oak Drive
Spring Arbor, MI 49283
drunyon@arbor.edu

Printed in the United States of America

Price: $28.50 USD

CONTENTS

INTRODUCTION

College Writing Models is the pain-free way to learn Modern Language Association (MLA) rules, page design, and Works Cited format. The text provides cross-references to the *MLA Handbook* and offers a simple sequence for creating college papers:

1. Read the chapter and literary model provided
2. Respond thoughtfully to the analysis questions
3. Outline and write a first draft paper based on current knowledge
4. Add depth and credibility based on targeted research and literature reviews
5. Consult the *MLA Handbook* to correctly document sources
6. Obtain peer reviewer guidance
7. Revise and polish the final draft.

This gives students the opportunity to explore their keen interests, control research, avoid plagiarism, and present their own arguments with power and persuasion.

The Strategy

College Writing Models is designed for composition courses at CCCU[1] and other educational institutions where faculty members desire to integrate Christian faith with academic pursuits. Most member schools have a general education curriculum designed to promote the

---

[1] The Council for Christian Colleges & Universities (CCCU) has 111 members in North America and 71 affiliate institutions, of which 43 are in other countries. The organization advances Christ-centered higher education and helps institutions transform lives by faithfully relating scholarship and service to biblical truth.

spiritual and intellectual development of servant-scholars with the knowledge and ability to think and act critically as Christians across disciplinary boundaries. This text accomplishes that vision by helping students encounter the Christian faith as they learn to understand and apply the concepts of a Christian worldview, develop an ability to think creatively and critically, and demonstrate proficiency in research writing while expressing ideas logically.

This text recognizes that the best way to learn to write is to read and imitate good writing. Since third person is often required in formal writing, the concepts in each chapter are explained in third person. Since instructions are usually given in second person, the text uses second person with the analysis questions, writing assignments, and peer review guidelines. The text deliberately shows students how to do everything expected of them.

Each chapter contains readings that model the type of writing under investigation so students first have a style of writing explained, then have that form of writing modeled, followed by assignments giving them opportunity to write in the same vein. Analysis questions after each reading are targeted to achieve Bloom's Taxonomy objectives of evaluation, synthesis, analysis, application, understanding, and knowledge (Dalton). Responding to the questions both aids students in comprehension and trains them to ask the kinds of questions useful when doing textual analysis.

Peer review exercises specific to each chapter function as a form of test marketing as students practice the art of connecting with their audience while engaging interactively in the writing process, which usually requires extensive editing and rewriting. Peer reviews also give students opportunity to teach others, an educational strategy recognizing that one effective way to learn a thing is to teach it.

This text builds from simple to more complex forms of writing while teaching research skills in a progressive fashion so students are not overwhelmed by the complexity of MLA documentation.[2] No attempt is made to give instruction on the fundamentals of grammar and punctuation since that is ably covered in the *MLA Stylebook,* and cross-references to that book are included.

The Foundation

"In the beginning was the Word" (John 1:1), the *logos*, the root of the English word "logic." A better source demonstrating how to think, and how to use words, will never exist. Using biblical passages to model effective writing makes sense from the practical standpoint because the Bible is the most widely read and continuously published book in the history of humankind. David Van Biema writes in *Time* magazine, "Not only is the Bible the best-selling book of all time, it is the best-selling book of the year every year," and students "need the Bible to make sense of the ideas and rhetoric that have helped drive U.S. history" (43).

T. R. Henn says the Bible provides the Western tradition with its "single greatest source" (258). Northrop Frye calls the Bible "the major informing influence on literary symbolism" (*Anatomy of Criticism* 316).[3] The symbols and images used in the Bible pervade western literature. Frye's list includes city, mountain, river, garden, tree, oil, fountain, bread, wine, bride, and sheep. These images "indicate some kind of unifying principle," and Frye identifies "a unified structure of narrative and imagery in the Bible" (*The Great Code: The Bible and Literature* xiii).[4] These critics are contending that knowledge of the Bible is essential to comprehending *any* western literature.

---

[2] Some disciplines require APA (American Psychological Association) documentation. Access <http://owl.english.purdue.edu/owl/resource> for comprehensive APA guidance.

[3] See also Leland Ryken, *The Literature of the Bible* (Grand Rapids: Zondervan, 1974), and Rene Wellek and Austin Warren, "The Nature of Literature," *Theory of Literature*, 3rd ed. (New York: Harcourt, Brace and World, 1956) 20-28.

[4] Frye's "Great Code" language comes from Blake, who said, "The Old and New Testaments are the Great Code of Art" (quoted in Frye xvi).

Students need knowledge of the Bible both for its content and for its presentation of that content, as Mark Twain explains: "It is hard to make a choice of the most beautiful passage in a book which is so gemmed with beautiful passages as the Bible.... Who taught those ancient writers their simplicity of language, their felicity of expression, their pathos, and above all, their faculty of sinking themselves entirely out of sight of the reader and making the narrative stand out alone and seem to tell itself?" (*The Innocents Abroad* 220).

The Bible is foundational for students interested in the art of literary criticism, and it is an effective tool for teaching writers in every discipline how to communicate both simple and complex thoughts. In addition to its interesting stories and great poetry, the Bible also contains timeless truth. Reading and thinking about the masterpieces modeled therein helps students become better people as well as better writers and thinkers.

The Assignments

All the literary models are accompanied by analysis questions that help students imprint what they have read into their memories by carrying on a written conversation with the author. Students should imagine the author as a personal friend talking directly to them over a delicious beverage. They can ask the author questions, thank him for wise advice, complain about what he has not said that they wish they knew, or mention related information they already know.

Student responses to the analysis questions demonstrate the ability to "think" on paper by responding quickly, yet sensibly, to ideas. Also, good writing is the result of continual rewriting, and student responses to analysis questions represent first thoughts and ideas that may develop into carefully crafted research papers. Just as art students look at model as they draw or paint, so writing students following *College Writing Models* will write something that resembles what they have just read. It makes sense that students would read a chapter about narrative writing, respond in writing to a sample narrative, and then write their own narrative. Students are invited to imitate—but not plagiarize—sample writings.[5]

Following the strategies outlined in this text helps teachers hold in check the proliferation of electronic file sharing and plagiarism common in the educational system today. Students must show the developmental path of their writing through their answers to analysis questions, their first draft of the actual writing assignment based on their current knowledge, their marked-up peer reviews, and their additions and refinements to the document resulting from research and written literature reviews.

Math teachers commonly tell students, "Don't just give the answers—show your work." *College Writing Models* is built around the same assumption—writing students must show their work as it progresses into a final draft that is both well crafted and uniquely their own.

---

[5] See *MLA Handbook* 2.1—2.8 for guidelines on how to avoid plagiarism.

CHAPTER 1: NARRATIVE

Narrative writing simply describes things as they are using agreed-upon facts. It answers these questions:

Questions	**Sample Answers**
Who was involved?	Zeke
What happened?	Started coloring
When did it happen?	When he was five years old
Where did it happen?	In kindergarten at Warner Elementary School
Why did it happen?	In obedience to Miss Miller
How did it happen?	Using a new box of crayons

The person who writes narrative works like a building's plumbing that does not influence the temperature or quality of the water. Plumbing merely delivers water. Users may conclude that "the water is hot," or "the water stinks," or "the water is delicious," but they are drawing their own conclusions based on successful delivery of facts by invisible yet essential plumbing. Writers who remain equally invisible achieve objectivity. Consider the differences between objective and subjective information:

Examples: **Opinion:** Yesterday morning it was cold outside.

Fact: Yesterday morning it was minus three degrees Fahrenheit outside.

Opinions are often so well accepted that they are recognized as fact in some cultures but need to be talked about in objective ways so that the audience is more receptive to the message:

Opinion: Jesus Christ is the Son of God.

Fact: Jesus Christ said he was the Son of God.

Attribution is the art of assigning all subjective information to its source and permitting readers to draw their own conclusions. The statement may or may not be fact, but it is a fact that the statement was made.

Fact: noun—truth; reality; a thing known for certain to have occurred or to be true; a datum of experience, events, or circumstances as distinct from its legal interpretation.

Bias: verb—cause to swerve from a course; influence (usually unfairly), inspire with prejudice. The art of narrative writing is to present facts in an unbiased way. The next chapter deals with descriptive writing, and it is important to recognize the differences now.

Subjective presentation of information is often used in descriptive writing, the subject of the next chapter. **Objective** presentation of information works well in narrative writing, the subject of this chapter.

ASSIGNMENT

Find a newspaper articles containing only unbiased narrative. Hint: It will probably be in the news section rather than on the editorial or sports pages. Use the distinctions given here:

Subjective (descriptive writing)	**Objective** (narrative writing)
Opinion: Exists only in the mind	Fact: Exists in nature. Known object.
Personal judgment	Real, outside of the mind
Result of feelings or temperament	Actual, independent of mind
Incapable of being checked externally	Without bias or prejudice
or verified by other people	Detached, impersonal

Remember, narrative writing simply describes things as they are using agreed-upon facts. Do not imagine narrative to be inherently boring. Narrative has a purpose and makes a point, often by portraying action and conflict. Either the first-person or third-person point of view is possible, but in college writing use third-person.

Use dialogue when possible to spice up a narrative. With this technique, opinion can slip through because it is attributed to a source other than the author. To write, "the dog is ugly," reveals author bias, but to write, "Maria said, 'the dog is ugly,'" maintains author objectivity.

NARRATIVE MODEL

Narrative writing derives from the oral tradition of storytelling. Note in the story below how carefully the narrator avoids expressing opinion and merely reports facts. Whenever an opinion is expressed, it is attributed to—and spoken by—one of the characters. Writers skilled in the art of attribution are able to present a story objectively while showing how the people influenced by the events of the narrative feel about what happens.

Ruth 1-4 (New Living Translation)

[1]In the days when the judges ruled in Israel, a man from Bethlehem in Judah left the country because of a severe famine. He took his wife and two sons and went to live in the country of Moab. [2]The man's name was Elimelech, and his wife was Naomi. Their two sons were Mahlon and Kilion. They were Ephrathites from Bethlehem in the land of Judah. During their stay in Moab, [3]Elimelech died and Naomi was left with her two sons. [4]The two sons married Moabite women. One married a woman named Orpah, and the other a woman named Ruth. But about ten years later, [5]both Mahlon and Kilion died. This left Naomi alone, without her husband or sons.

[6]Then Naomi heard in Moab that the LORD had blessed his people in Judah by giving them good crops again. So Naomi and her daughters-in-law got ready to leave Moab to return to her

homeland. [7]With her two daughters-in-law she set out from the place where she had been living, and they took the road that would lead them back to Judah.

[8]But on the way, Naomi said to her two daughters-in-law, "Go back to your mothers' homes instead of coming with me. And may the LORD reward you for your kindness to your husbands and to me. [9]May the LORD bless you with the security of another marriage." Then she kissed them good-bye, and they all broke down and wept.

[10]"No," they said. "We want to go with you to your people."

[11]But Naomi replied, "Why should you go on with me? Can I still give birth to other sons who could grow up to be your husbands? [12]No, my daughters, return to your parents' homes, for I am too old to marry again. And even if it were possible, and I were to get married tonight and bear sons, then what? [13]Would you wait for them to grow up and refuse to marry someone else? No, of course not, my daughters! Things are far more bitter for me than for you, because the LORD himself has caused me to suffer."

[14]And again they wept together, and Orpah kissed her mother-in-law good-bye. But Ruth insisted on staying with Naomi. [15]"See," Naomi said to her, "your sister-in-law has gone back to her people and to her gods. You should do the same."

[16]But Ruth replied, "Don't ask me to leave you and turn back. I will go wherever you go and live wherever you live. Your people will be my people, and your God will be my God. [17]I will die where you die and will be buried there. May the LORD punish me severely if I allow anything but death to separate us!" [18]So when Naomi saw that Ruth had made up her mind to go with her, she stopped urging her.

[19]So the two of them continued on their journey. When they came to Bethlehem, the entire town was stirred by their arrival. "Is it really Naomi?" the women asked.

[20]"Don't call me Naomi," she told them. "Instead, call me Mara, for the Almighty has made
life very bitter for me. [21]I went away full, but the LORD has brought me home empty. Why
should you call me Naomi when the LORD has caused me to suffer and the Almighty has sent
such tragedy?"

[22]So Naomi returned from Moab, accompanied by her daughter-in-law Ruth, the young
Moabite woman. They arrived in Bethlehem at the beginning of the barley harvest.

Ruth 2

[1]Now there was a wealthy and influential man in Bethlehem named Boaz, who was a relative
of Naomi's husband, Elimelech.

[2]One day Ruth said to Naomi, "Let me go out into the fields to gather leftover grain behind
anyone who will let me do it."

And Naomi said, "All right, my daughter, go ahead." [3]So Ruth went out to gather grain
behind the harvesters. And as it happened, she found herself working in a field that belonged to
Boaz, the relative of her father-in-law, Elimelech.

[4]While she was there, Boaz arrived from Bethlehem and greeted the harvesters. "The LORD
be with you!" he said.

"The LORD bless you!" the harvesters replied.

[5]Then Boaz asked his foreman, "Who is that girl over there?"

[6]And the foreman replied, "She is the young woman from Moab who came back with Naomi.
[7]She asked me this morning if she could gather grain behind the harvesters. She has been hard at
work ever since, except for a few minutes' rest over there in the shelter."

[8]Boaz went over and said to Ruth, "Listen, my daughter. Stay right here with us when you
gather grain; don't go to any other fields. Stay right behind the women working in my field. [9]See

which part of the field they are harvesting, and then follow them. I have warned the young men not to bother you. And when you are thirsty, help yourself to the water they have drawn from the well."

[10]Ruth fell at his feet and thanked him warmly. "Why are you being so kind to me?" she asked. "I am only a foreigner."

[11]"Yes, I know," Boaz replied. "But I also know about the love and kindness you have shown your mother-in-law since the death of your husband. I have heard how you left your father and mother and your own land to live here among complete strangers. [12]May the LORD, the God of Israel, under whose wings you have come to take refuge, reward you fully."

[13]"I hope I continue to please you, sir," she replied. "You have comforted me by speaking so kindly to me, even though I am not as worthy as your workers."

[14]At lunchtime Boaz called to her, "Come over here and help yourself to some of our food. You can dip your bread in the wine if you like." So she sat with his harvesters, and Boaz gave her food—more than she could eat.

[15]When Ruth went back to work again, Boaz ordered his young men, "Let her gather grain right among the sheaves without stopping her. [16]And pull out some heads of barley from the bundles and drop them on purpose for her. Let her pick them up, and don't give her a hard time!"

[17]So Ruth gathered barley there all day, and when she beat out the grain that evening, it came to about half a bushel. [18]She carried it back into town and showed it to her mother-in-law. Ruth also gave her the food that was left over from her lunch.

[19]"So much!" Naomi exclaimed. "Where did you gather all this grain today? Where did you work? May the LORD bless the one who helped you!"

So Ruth told her mother-in-law about the man in whose field she had worked. And she said, "The man I worked with today is named Boaz."

[20]"May the LORD bless him!" Naomi told her daughter-in-law. "He is showing his kindness to us as well as to your dead husband. That man is one of our closest relatives, one of our family redeemers."

[21]Then Ruth said, "What's more, Boaz even told me to come back and stay with his harvesters until the entire harvest is completed."

[22]"This is wonderful!" Naomi exclaimed. "Do as he said. Stay with his workers right through the whole harvest. You will be safe there, unlike in other fields."

[23]So Ruth worked alongside the women in Boaz's fields and gathered grain with them until the end of the barley harvest. Then she worked with them through the wheat harvest, too. But all the while she lived with her mother-in-law.

Ruth 3

[1]One day Naomi said to Ruth, "My daughter, it's time that I found a permanent home for you, so that you will be provided for. [2]Boaz is a close relative of ours, and he's been very kind by letting you gather grain with his workers. Tonight he will be winnowing barley at the threshing floor. [3]Now do as I tell you—take a bath and put on perfume and dress in your nicest clothes. Then go to the threshing floor, but don't let Boaz see you until he has finished his meal. [4]Be sure to notice where he lies down; then go and uncover his feet and lie down there. He will tell you what to do."

[5]"I will do everything you say," Ruth replied. [6]So she went down to the threshing floor that night and followed the instructions of her mother-in-law.

[7]After Boaz had finished his meal and was in good spirits, he lay down beside the heap of grain and went to sleep. Then Ruth came quietly, uncovered his feet, and lay down. [8]Around midnight, Boaz suddenly woke up and turned over. He was surprised to find a woman lying at his feet! [9]"Who are you?" he demanded.

"I am your servant Ruth," she replied. "Spread the corner of your covering over me, for you are my family redeemer."

[10]"The LORD bless you, my daughter!" Boaz exclaimed. "You are showing more family loyalty now than ever by not running after a younger man, whether rich or poor. [11]Now don't worry about a thing, my daughter. I will do what is necessary, for everyone in town knows you are an honorable woman. [12]But there is one problem. While it is true that I am one of your family redeemers, there is another man who is more closely related to you than I am. [13]Stay here tonight, and in the morning I will talk to him. If he is willing to redeem you, then let him marry you. But if he is not willing, then as surely as the LORD lives, I will marry you! Now lie down here until morning."

[14]So Ruth lay at Boaz's feet until the morning, but she got up before it was light enough for people to recognize each other. For Boaz said, "No one must know that a woman was here at the threshing floor." [15]Boaz also said to her, "Bring your cloak and spread it out." He measured out six scoops of barley into the cloak and helped her put it on her back. Then Boaz returned to the town.

[16]When Ruth went back to her mother-in-law, Naomi asked, "What happened, my daughter?"

Ruth told Naomi everything Boaz had done for her, [17]and she added, "He gave me these six scoops of barley and said, 'Don't go back to your mother-in-law empty-handed.'"

[18]Then Naomi said to her, "Just be patient, my daughter, until we hear what happens. The man won't rest until he has followed through on this. He will settle it today."

Ruth 4

[1]So Boaz went to the town gate and took a seat there. When the family redeemer he had mentioned came by, Boaz called out to him, "Come over here, friend. I want to talk to you." So they sat down together. [2]Then Boaz called ten leaders from the town and asked them to sit as witnesses. [3]And Boaz said to the family redeemer, "You know Naomi, who came back from Moab. She is selling the land that belonged to our relative Elimelech. [4]I felt that I should speak to you about it so that you can redeem it if you wish. If you want the land, then buy it here in the presence of these witnesses. But if you don't want it, let me know right away, because I am next in line to redeem it after you."

The man replied, "All right, I'll redeem it."

[5]Then Boaz told him, "Of course, your purchase of the land from Naomi also requires that you marry Ruth, the Moabite widow. That way, she can have children who will carry on her husband's name and keep the land in the family."

[6]"Then I can't redeem it," the family redeemer replied, "because this might endanger my own estate. You redeem the land; I cannot do it."

[7]In those days it was the custom in Israel for anyone transferring a right of purchase to remove his sandal and hand it to the other party. This publicly validated the transaction. [8]So the other family redeemer drew off his sandal as he said to Boaz, "You buy the land."

[9]Then Boaz said to the leaders and to the crowd standing around, "You are witnesses that today I have bought from Naomi all the property of Elimelech, Kilion, and Mahlon. [10]And with the land I have acquired Ruth, the Moabite widow of Mahlon, to be my wife. This way she can

have a son to carry on the family name of her dead husband and to inherit the family property here in his hometown. You are all witnesses today."

11 Then the leaders and all the people standing there replied, "We are witnesses! May the LORD make the woman who is now coming into your home like Rachel and Leah, from whom all the nation of Israel descended! May you be great in Ephrathah and famous in Bethlehem. 12 And may the LORD give you descendants by this young woman who will be like those of our ancestor Perez, the son of Tamar and Judah."

13 So Boaz married Ruth and took her home to live with him. When he slept with her, the LORD enabled her to become pregnant, and she gave birth to a son. 14 And the women of the town said to Naomi, "Praise the LORD who has given you a family redeemer today! May he be famous in Israel. 15 May this child restore your youth and care for you in your old age. For he is the son of your daughter-in-law who loves you so much and who has been better to you than seven sons!"

16 Naomi took care of the baby and cared for him as if he were her own. 17 The neighbor women said, "Now at last Naomi has a son again!" And they named him Obed. He became the father of Jesse and the grandfather of David.

18 This is their family line beginning with their ancestor Perez: Perez was the father of Hezron. 19 Hezron was the father of Ram. Ram was the father of Amminadab. 20 Amminadab was the father of Nahshon. Nahshon was the father of Salmon. 21 Salmon was the father of Boaz. Boaz was the father of Obed. 22 Obed was the father of Jesse. Jesse was the father of David.

ANALYSIS QUESTIONS

Write a paragraph of response to each question below. The questions are designed to introduce you to the art of literary criticism and analysis using Bloom's Taxonomy, which provides opportunity to demonstrate your knowledge, comprehension, application, analysis, synthesis, and evaluation of the reading model (Dalton).

Write your responses in the form of a letter or casual conversation with the author of the narrative. It may be easier if you imagine the author is a personal friend, relative, or college roommate. Your responses will serve as a form of pre-writing to help you master narrative style and prepare you to write a narrative of your own.

1. Search for a spot in the narrative where the author expresses an opinion. If you can find such an expression, explain whether it is appropriate or inappropriate given the context.
2. What is Ruth's opinion of Boaz? How do you know?
3. What is Naomi's opinion of Ruth? How do you know?
4. What do you think is the author's purpose in narrating the story of Ruth?
5. Showing action is important in many narratives. In your opinion, what is the most exciting action that takes place in this story? Give details. Why do you like it?
6. What are the issues behind the main conflict in this narrative? Give details.
7. From what point of view is this story told? How would the story feel differently if it were told from the point of view of Boaz?
8. Dialogue is used in this story to reveal character. In what ways do you feel you know Ruth better because you have "heard" her talk?
9. Compare this story with the news article from the page 7 assignment. What is the bias of each author? (See *MLA Handbook* 5.7.5 for how to document a newspaper article; see *MLA Handbook* 6.4.8 for how to document a Bible passage.)
10. What techniques of narrative writing have you learned from Ruth that may be useful for writing your own narrative?

WRITING ASSIGNMENT

It is time to write your own narrative. Write this paper on a topic about which you are passionate. This topic will most likely fall within the area of your academic major. For example, most psychology majors are particularly interested in a specific psychological phenomenon. Natural science majors want to study biology, or chemistry, or geology, or physics. Music students may be focused on Baroque or Jazz or another genre of music, or on a favorite composer. If you have not declared a major, focus on something you could enjoy studying in great depth—a favorite thing to think about—a topic so fascinating you could write 35 pages without getting *bored*. Identify your topic here:

____

____

As you write, follow these guidelines:

1. A narrative relates a series of events. **Assignment:** Write a narrative containing a series of events that influenced you to embrace the interest that you have.
2. A narrative makes a point or has a purpose. **Assignment:** State the purpose of your narrative.
3. Action plays a central role in any narrative. **Assignment:** Show lots of action in your narrative.
4. A narrative needs a point of view. **Assignment:** Even though the narrative is about yourself, adopt a third-person point of view as your narrative style. Follow the example of the Ruth narrative.
5. Good narrative uses dialogue. **Assignment:** Include at least one brief conversation using quote marks and paragraphing as modeled in the *MLA Handbook* (look up "quotes" in the index for guidelines on how to format and punctuate dialogue).

Remember: the narrative itself must be objective, but subjective material can be attributed to a character who expresses opinion in the form of dialogue.

6. Now imagine you are talking to a stranger who knows little about your topic. Use very simple language to explain your topic to that person. Answer the journalist's questions in your narrative: who, what, when, where, why, how?
7. Write a one-page narrative based on what you already know about the topic.

TROUBLE?

If you had trouble with this exercise or discovered that you want to write about something not within your college major, do not panic. Remember, "We have different gifts, according to the grace given us. . . . [Let us] use it in proportion to [our] faith" (Rom. 12:6). Alexander Borodin was a nineteenth-century Russian composer, a member of "The Mighty Handful," a group of composers dedicated to producing Russian music. His opera, *Prince Igor*, is thought by some to have been his most significant work, but Borodin was an organic chemist! He considered himself merely a "Sunday composer" ("AlexanderBorodin").

Similarly, Socrates was a stonemason who asked questions and challenged people to think. Today he is remembered as the founder of Western philosophical thought (Carr). Alexander Graham Bell was a teacher whose wife was nearly deaf, and he invented the telephone trying to help her hear better ("Alexander Graham Bell"). The Wright brothers built bicycles in Ohio but fiddled around with the idea of flying—just as a sideline ("The Wright Story").

You are a complex person with many talents and interests. You have no idea what you will become. But one way to get there is to begin now using God-given talents to write concerning things you are passionate about. What is your deepest dream? Write a narrative concerning that dream—even if you presume that achieving it is impossible.

(name of person writing review) ___________________________________

PEER REVIEW: Valuable insights often result when a fellow student reads and evaluates the narrative. Even readers who are not qualified as editors can serve as an audience for the narrative, and their responses can guide the author to make refinements.

____ The entire narrative must be written from the third-person point of view. Circle all first and second person pronouns and make suggestions to help the writer get it all in third person.

1ST Person Pronouns (avoid these)	2nd Person Pronouns (avoid these)	3rd Person Pronouns (use these)
I, me, my	you, your	he, she, him, her
we, us, our	you, y'all	they, them, their, those

Hint: One easy way to write in third person is to choose plural subjects for sentences so third person plural pronouns can be used. **Example:** Instead of "The child takes his/her lunch to school in a sack," write "The children take their lunches to school in sacks."

____ Search through the narrative again, this time looking for evidence that all six questions have been adequately answered (who, what, when, where, why, how?).

____ Evaluate the structure to make sure the six questions have been answered in the order the reader is likely to ask them. Also, some of the questions get answered over and over again at increasing levels of significance.

____ "Place brackets [ ] to identify all dialogue," he suggested, "and make sure quote marks and punctuation are done correctly." (See MLA 3.7.7 "Punctuation with Quotations" for guidelines.)

____ Identify incorrect use of commas so the author can make corrections (See MLA 3.2.2 "Commas" for guidelines).

Answer the following questions:

____What is the main point of this narrative? ____

____What is the biggest strength? ____

____What material does not fit the main point or the audience? _____________________________

____ What questions has the author not answered? ______________________________________

____

____ At what point does the paper fail to hold my interest? ______________________________

Why? ____

____ Where is the organization confusing? ____

____ Where is the writing unclear or vague? ____

On the back of your classmate's paper, write a note to the author explaining what you enjoyed most about reading this narrative.

Research Time

____ Where should more facts be added to give this paper more credibility?

____ Suggest a source where this author might look up more information that would strengthen the content of this paper.

____ Write a few reasons why this paper would be better if it had the facts and information suggested in the above questions.

PLANNING THE REWRITE

The first draft seldom reflects a writer's best work. The peer review usually reveals a few ways the first draft can be improved. Consider the suggestions of the peer reviewer, and also read *MLA Handbook* 1.9 "Writing Drafts" and 3.1-3.8 "The Mechanics of Writing" for rewriting suggestions.

Write the final draft on computer and format it according to instructions in the *MLA Handbook* Chapter 4: "The Format of the Research Paper" (115-122) with header and page number, title, double spacing, and other exact details. Use a Times New Roman 12-point font and one-inch margins. Finally, locate additional information that will strengthen the content of the paper while providing facts and sources that will enhance your credibility. Writing a literature review as explained below will create the research needed.

LITERATURE REVIEW

Add in-depth details to your narrative following these guidelines: Go to the reference desk of your library and locate a *subject* (specialized) encyclopedia specific to the topic of your paper. Locate an article on your topic and fill in the information requested below:

Author (if given): ______________________________

Title of article: ______________________________

Title of Encyclopedia: ______________________________

Call Number of Encyclopedia: ______________________________

Is there a bibliography at the end of the article? __✓__ yes ____ no

Read the entries related to your topic in the reference book you have chosen and take notes useful to the paper. Use this information to create a literature review by indirect and direct quotations as explained below.

An **indirect quotation** presents an author's ideas through *paraphrasing* or *summarizing*. **Example**: Ending a sentence with a preposition is an older rule that has, to some extent, been done away with (Strunk and White 77). The idea has been rewritten in words not used by the original author, so it must be referenced. Using indirect quotations indicates that the author clearly understands the information and can smoothly integrate it into an argument.

Paraphrasing means rewriting someone else's idea using different words. A paraphrase is usually about the same length as the original. Compare the Living Bible paraphrase with the New International Version translation: "And the Holy Spirit helps us in our distress. For we don't even know what we should pray for, nor how we should pray. But the Holy Spirit prays for us with groanings that cannot be expressed in words" (Rom. 8:26). The above paraphrase gets across the same idea as the following careful translation from the Greek: "In the same way, the Spirit helps us in our weakness. We do not know what we ought to pray for, but the Spirit himself intercedes for us with groans that words cannot express" (Rom. 8:26 NIV).

Summarizing is a form of indirect quotation, but is much shorter than the original text. A summary encapsulates the essence or main point. **Example:** The Apostle Paul argues in Romans 8:26 that the Holy Spirit mysteriously helps believers to pray effectively.

A **direct quotation** transcribes an author's words from the text using the *exact* wording (including mistakes). Use direct quotations sparingly—only when they make a precise point and are both brief and substantial. **Example:** "Years ago, students were warned not to end a sentence with a preposition; time, of course, has softened that rigid decree" (Strunk and White 77).

Now that the differences are clear between indirect quotation (paraphrasing and summarizing) and direct quotation, do the following:

1. **Paraphrase** a key paragraph of the article being careful to avoid plagiarism as explained in the *MLA Handbook* 2.5.

2. **Summarize** the article or a key part of the article entirely in your own words.

3. **Quote** one excellent sentence by carefully copying it into your paper. Put quote marks around the quote and insert an appropriate introduction such as, Blanchard writes, "Never eat olives after midnight or you'll get cramps."

To find out what information to put in a Works Cited entry to accompany the above paraphrase, summary, and quote, look up "encyclopedia articles" in the index of the *MLA Handbook* (page 273). The index entry will refer you to other sections of the *MLA Handbook* (in this case page 160, "An Article in a Reference Book.") When you have found the correct format to follow, write the information from your article into a Works Cited entry at the end of your paper *in exactly the correct format.*

PARENTHETICAL REFERENCE

Now look at the *MLA* index to find the entry concerning "encyclopedia articles . . . in parenthetical references" and "encyclopedias, as reference sources" to find out how to create a parenthetical reference for your indirect and direct quotes. Insert the parenthetical references at the end of your paraphrase, summary, and quote *in the correct format.*

Guidelines on how to gracefully integrate the new research with the paper you have written are provided in chapter six of the *MLA Handbook.* Pay particular attention to section 6.3 beginning on page 216. In addition to those instructions, be sure to create a context that shows the reader precisely how this new material is an integral part of your paper.

Include a Works Cited page with your paper. The format should use double spacing, hanging indentation, alphabetical order, and look exactly like the Works Cited page at the end of this book. Note that although you will have three or more parenthetical references in the body of your paper, there will be only one Works Cited entry, since all your parenthetical references are to that one source.

When you have made all the needed corrections to your paper, when it is typed without errors and formatted according to MLA guidelines, when you can genuinely say you are proud of this writing—this piece of yourself—and (of course) when the teacher says it is due, turn in the narrative for evaluation and grading. No matter what grade the manuscript receives, celebrate the fact that with your words you have spoken a new creation into existence, and you have done all in your power to make it "very good."[1]

---

[1] Gen. 1:31: "God saw all that he had made [spoken into existence], and it was very good."

CHAPTER 2: DESCRIPTION

Narrative writing, explored in the previous chapter, is efficient and respectable as it tells a story and lets the facts speak. Good writers master the art of narrative, and also know when to go beyond it with description. **Descriptive writing** takes a pause in the narrative to look in detail at a particular feature. It can bore or inspire the reader depending on the author's skill. Edward George Bulwer-Lytton's character Pelham plunges into description as he attempts to capture the beauty of a woman he eventually marries:[1]

> Never had I seen any countenance half so lovely. She was apparently about twenty, her hair was of the richest chestnut, and a golden light played through its darkness, as if a sunbeam had been caught in those luxuriant tresses, and was striving in vain to escape. Her eyes were of a light hazel, large, deep, and *shaded into softness* (to use a modern expression) by long and very dark lashes. Her complexion alone would have rendered her beautiful, it was so clear—so pure; the blood blushed beneath it, like roses under a clear stream; if, in order to justify my simile, roses would have the complacency to grow in such a situation. Her nose was of that fine and accurate mould that one so seldom sees, except in the Grecian statues, which unites the clearest and most decided outline with the most feminine delicacy and softness, and the short curved arch which descended from thence to

[1] Published in 1828, *Pelham* was a popular English novel that introduced to society dark evening wear for men (the tuxedo). Archaic punctuation in this quote is maintained exactly as the original, even though it does not reflect current MLA style.

> her mouth, was so fine—so *airily* and exquisitely formed, that it seemed as if Love himself had modelled the bridge which led to his most beautiful and fragrant island. On the right side of the mouth was one dimple, that corresponded so exactly with every smile and movement of those rosy lips, that you might have sworn the shadow of each passed there; it was like the rapid changes of an April heaven reflected upon a valley. She was somewhat, but not much taller, than the ordinary height; and her figure, which united all the first freshness and youth of the girl, with the more luxuriant graces of the woman, was rounded and finished so justly—so *minutely*—that the eye could glance over the whole, without discovering the least harshness, or unevenness, or atom, to be added or subtracted. But over all these was a light, a glow, a pervading spirit, of which it is impossible to convey the faintest idea. You should have seen her by the side of a shaded fountain on a summer's day. You should have watched her amidst music and flowers…. (166-167)

The art of description is to know when enough is enough. If the reader begs, "Please!—get on with the story," the author is using too much description. If the reader smiles and thinks, "I love it when we stop and smell the roses," this author has fostered the intended vicarious experience.

Descriptive writing can also sprinkle itself throughout narrative with carefully placed adjectives (describing words). Profane and vulgar terms are adjectives, and students often ask if such words are appropriate in academic writing. The answer is "no," and authors who stoop to such language are frequently abandoning the creative instinct. A better model is Mark Twain's technique in *Life on the Mississippi* of simulating such language: [2]

---

[2] Note that although MLA specifies that "whang" should use double quote marks, single marks are used here to faithfully reproduce the original text.

> All of a sudden, on a murky night, a light would hop up, right under our bows, almost, and an agonized voice, with the backwoods 'whang' to it, would wail out—
>
> 'War'n the—you goin' to! Cain't you see nothin', you dash-dashed aig-suckin', sheep-stealin', one-eyed son of a stuffed monkey!' (71-72)

Notice that Twain is using slang to achieve his vulgarity objectives. This is the creative and acceptable alternative to using profanity. In "A Defence of Slang" G. K. Chesterton writes that slang is metaphor: "If we … examine the cheapest cant phrases that pass our lips every day, we should find that they were as rich and suggestive as so many sonnets" (146). Be sure to explain the meaning of slang expressions within the context, as John Bunyan does in *The Holy War.* When Lord Willbewill apprehends Evil-questioning, the villain is entertaining four "doubters" described as "down boys, you have the very length of my foot." This expression is interpreted in the next phrase when Evil-questioning admits that the doubters "are one with my heart" (235).

Simulated profanity can also be handled using adjectives the way Hemingway does in *For Whom the Bell Tolls* when the barbarous "woman of Pablo" says to the gypsy, "What are you doing now, you lazy drunken obscene unsayable son of an unnameable unmarried gypsy obscenity?" (34). Whether in separate passages of description or in adjective-laced narrative, descriptive writing uses all five senses: taste, touch, smell, sight, and sound.

Descriptive writing is particularly effective when many sensations flood together so that the reader seems to *taste* colors, *feel* music, *smell* anger, *see* ideas, or *hear* the sunset. "Synaesthesia" is "The production of a mental sense-impression relating to one sense by the stimulation of another sense, as in coloured hearing. Also, a sensation produced in one part of the body by stimulation of another part." In linguistics it is possible to transfer "the meaning of a word from one kind of sensory experience to another" (OED).

Descriptive writing works to trigger synaesthesia. In a long passage describing steamboat racing in *Life on the Mississippi*, Mark Twain achieves synaesthesia when he describes a frantic scene obscured by clouds of words: "Drays and baggage-vans were clattering hither and thither in a wild hurry, every now and then getting blocked and jammed together, and then during ten seconds one could not see them for the profanity…" (116).

The art of descriptive writing is beautifully illustrated in *Teaching a Stone to Talk* where Annie Dillard relates her experience near the Napo River in the Ecuadorian jungle: "Green fireflies spattered lights across the air and illumined for seconds, now here, now there, the pale trunks of enormous, solitary trees. Beneath us the brown Napo River was rising, in all silence; it coiled up the sandy bank and tangled its foam in vines that trailed from the forest and roots that looped the shore" (54). Having described the setting, Dillard now immerses her reader in a powerful experience of touch:

> Later that night I loosed my hair from its braids and combed it smooth—not for myself, but so the village girls could play with it in the morning…. I had slumped on some shaded steps, wishing I knew some Spanish or some Quechua so I could speak with the ring of little girls who were alternately staring at me and smiling at their toes. I spoke anyway, and fooled with my hair, which they were obviously dying to get their hands on, and laughed, and soon they were all braiding my hair, all five of them, all fifty fingers, all my hair, even my bangs. And then they took it apart and did it again, laughing, and teaching me Spanish nouns, and meeting my eyes and each other's with open delight…. (54-55)

The reader who wants to get his own hands into Annie's hair has been seduced by wonderful descriptive writing that embraces the senses. Seduction? Yes, and also a taste of heaven as C. S. Lewis explains in *Letters to Malcolm: Chiefly on Prayer*:

> But for our body one whole realm of God's glory—all that we receive through the senses—would go unpraised. For the beasts can't appreciate it and the angels are, I suppose, pure intelligences. They *understand* colours and tastes better than our greatest scientists; but have they retinas or palates? I fancy the 'beauties of nature'[3] are a secret God has shared with us alone. That may be one of the reasons why we were made—and why the resurrection of the body is an important doctrine. (17-18)

At the conclusion of his last book, C. S. Lewis affirmed, "What the soul cries out for is the resurrection of the senses" (*Letters to Malcolm* 121). If the five senses are to play such a vital role in human life eternally, surely they should be embraced in the literature of the present world—especially in writings that anticipate such glory.

DESCRIPTION MODELS

The book of Judges provides a dramatic model for how to follow narrative with description. Notice that chapter four is almost pure narrative, reading much like a news article revealing little bias. By contrast, chapter five celebrates the events of the previous narrative, immersing the reader in descriptions of the sorrow of death and the elation of victory.

Judges 4: Narrative (New International Version)

1 After Ehud died, the Israelites once again did evil in the eyes of the LORD. 2 So the
LORD sold them into the hands of Jabin, a king of Canaan, who reigned in Hazor. The

---

[3] The single quote marks around "beauties of nature" reflect a practice that persists among British authors although MLA calls for double quote marks.

commander of his army was Sisera, who lived in Harosheth Haggoyim. 3 Because he had nine hundred iron chariots and had cruelly oppressed the Israelites for twenty years, they cried to the LORD for help.

4 Deborah, a prophetess, the wife of Lappidoth, was leading Israel at that time. 5 She held court under the Palm of Deborah between Ramah and Bethel in the hill country of Ephraim, and the Israelites came to her to have their disputes decided. 6 She sent for Barak son of Abinoam from Kedesh in Naphtali and said to him, "The LORD, the God of Israel, commands you: 'Go, take with you ten thousand men of Naphtali and Zebulun and lead the way to Mount Tabor. 7 I will lure Sisera, the commander of Jabin's army, with his chariots and his troops to the Kishon River and give him into your hands.' "

8 Barak said to her, "If you go with me, I will go; but if you don't go with me, I won't go."

9 "Very well," Deborah said, "I will go with you. But because of the way you are going about this, the honor will not be yours, for the LORD will hand Sisera over to a woman." So Deborah went with Barak to Kedesh, 10 where he summoned Zebulun and Naphtali. Ten thousand men followed him, and Deborah also went with him.

11 Now Heber the Kenite had left the other Kenites, the descendants of Hobab, Moses' brother-in-law, and pitched his tent by the great tree in Zaanannim near Kedesh.

12 When they told Sisera that Barak son of Abinoam had gone up to Mount Tabor, 13 Sisera gathered together his nine hundred iron chariots and all the men with him, from Harosheth Haggoyim to the Kishon River.

14 Then Deborah said to Barak, "Go! This is the day the LORD has given Sisera into your hands. Has not the LORD gone ahead of you?" So Barak went down Mount Tabor, followed by ten thousand men. 15 At Barak's advance, the LORD routed Sisera and all his chariots and army by the sword, and Sisera abandoned his chariot and fled on foot. 16 But Barak pursued the

chariots and army as far as Harosheth Haggoyim. All the troops of Sisera fell by the sword; not a man was left.

17 Sisera, however, fled on foot to the tent of Jael, the wife of Heber the Kenite, because there were friendly relations between Jabin king of Hazor and the clan of Heber the Kenite.

18 Jael went out to meet Sisera and said to him, "Come, my Lord, come right in. Don't be afraid." So he entered her tent, and she put a covering over him.

19 "I'm thirsty," he said. "Please give me some water." She opened a skin of milk, gave him a drink, and covered him up.

20 "Stand in the doorway of the tent," he told her. "If someone comes by and asks you, 'Is anyone here?' say 'No.' "

21 But Jael, Heber's wife, picked up a tent peg and a hammer and went quietly to him while he lay fast asleep, exhausted. She drove the peg through his temple into the ground, and he died.

22 Barak came by in pursuit of Sisera, and Jael went out to meet him. "Come," she said, "I will show you the man you're looking for." So he went in with her, and there lay Sisera with the tent peg through his temple—dead.

23 On that day God subdued Jabin, the Canaanite king, before the Israelites. 24 And the
hand of the Israelites grew stronger and stronger against Jabin, the Canaanite king, until they
destroyed him.

ANALYSIS QUESTIONS

1. Discuss the efficiency with which the writer of Judges 4 covers the basic narrative questions of who, what, when, where, why, and how.
2. Suppose that your local newspaper had existed in the time of the Judges. Write a headline for that publication's front story article about this event.

3. Explain the ways a news article would be both similar and different from that reported in Judges 4.

Judges 5: Mainly Description (NIV) ***The Song of Deborah***

1 On that day Deborah and Barak son of Abinoam sang this song: 2 "When the princes in Israel take the lead, when the people willingly offer themselves—praise the LORD! 3 Hear this, you kings! Listen, you rulers! I will sing to the LORD, I will sing; I will make music to the LORD, the God of Israel.

4 "O LORD, when you went out from Seir, when you marched from the land of Edom, the earth shook, the heavens poured, the clouds poured down water. 5 The mountains quaked before the LORD, the One of Sinai, before the LORD, the God of Israel.

6 "In the days of Shamgar son of Anath, in the days of Jael, the roads were abandoned; travelers took to winding paths. 7 Village life in Israel ceased, ceased until I, Deborah, arose, arose a mother in Israel. 8 When they chose new gods, war came to the city gates, and not a shield or spear was seen among forty thousand in Israel. 9 My heart is with Israel's princes, with the willing volunteers among the people. Praise the LORD!

10 "You who ride on white donkeys, sitting on your saddle blankets, and you who walk along the road, consider 11 the voice of the singers at the watering places. They recite the righteous acts of the LORD, the righteous acts of his warriors in Israel.

"Then the people of the LORD went down to the city gates. 12 'Wake up, wake up, Deborah! Wake up, wake up, break out in song! Arise, O Barak! Take captive your captives, O son of Abinoam.'

13 "Then the men who were left came down to the nobles; the people of the LORD came to me with the mighty. 14 Some came from Ephraim, whose roots were in Amalek; Benjamin was

with the people who followed you. From Makir captains came down, from Zebulun those who bear a commander's staff. [15] The princes of Issachar were with Deborah; yes, Issachar was with Barak, rushing after him into the valley.

"In the districts of Reuben there was much searching of heart. [16] Why did you stay among the campfires to hear the whistling for the flocks? In the districts of Reuben there was much searching of heart. [17] Gilead stayed beyond the Jordan. And Dan, why did he linger by the ships? Asher remained on the coast and stayed in his coves. [18] The people of Zebulun risked their very lives; so did Naphtali on the heights of the field.

[19] "Kings came, they fought; the kings of Canaan fought at Taanach by the waters of Megiddo, but they carried off no silver, no plunder. [20] From the heavens the stars fought, from their courses they fought against Sisera. [21] The river Kishon swept them away, the age-old river, the river Kishon. March on, my soul; be strong! [22] Then thundered the horses' hoofs—galloping, galloping go his mighty steeds. [23] 'Curse Meroz,' said the angel of the LORD. 'Curse its people bitterly, because they did not come to help the LORD, to help the LORD against the mighty.'

[24] "Most blessed of women be Jael, the wife of Heber the Kenite, most blessed of tent-dwelling women. [25] He asked for water, and she gave him milk; in a bowl fit for nobles she brought him curdled milk. [26] Her hand reached for the tent peg, her right hand for the workman's hammer. She struck Sisera, she crushed his head, she shattered and pierced his temple. [27] At her feet he sank, he fell; there he lay. At her feet he sank, he fell; where he sank, there he fell—dead.

[28] "Through the window peered Sisera's mother; behind the lattice she cried out, 'Why is his chariot so long in coming? Why is the clatter of his chariots delayed?' [29] The wisest of her ladies answer her; indeed, she keeps saying to herself, [30] 'Are they not finding and dividing the spoils: a girl or two for each man, colorful garments as plunder for Sisera, colorful garments embroidered, highly embroidered garments for my neck—all this as plunder?'

31 "So may all your enemies perish, O LORD! But may they who love you be like the sun when it rises in its strength." Then the land had peace forty years.

ANALYSIS QUESTIONS

4. Which of the five senses (taste, touch, smell, sight, sound) is dominant in Deborah's description of the conflict? Speculate on why this may be deliberate.
5. Imagine you are peer reviewing Deborah's description. Which of the five senses do you wish she would explore more thoroughly? Write a sentence or two that you can recommend for inclusion in case she ever revises her paper.
6. Make a list of at least five ways in which Judges 5 is different from Judges 4.
7. Which version of the conflict do you like better, the narrative in Judges 4, or the more descriptive Song of Deborah in Judges 5? Why?

METAPHOR AS DESCRIPTION

In addition to modeling how to talk about the same event with separate narratives and descriptions, the Bible also uses metaphor to enhance the way a hing is described. A metaphor is a symbol of some other (usually abstract) thing. To say that the university library is a "hive of activity" is a metaphor.[4] Hebrews 1:7 reads, "And of the angels He says: '*Who makes His angels spirits and His ministers a flame of fire,"* and verses 10-12 read as follows:

> You, LORD, in the beginning laid the foundation of the earth,
>
> And the heavens are the work of Your hands.
>
> They will perish, but You remain;
>
> And they will all grow old like a garment;
>
> Like a cloak You will fold them up,

---

[4] English teachers often say, "A metaphor is a comparison between two people, places, or things without the use of *like* or *as*."

And they will be changed.

But You are the same,

And Your years will not fail.

The writer who combines metaphor with the five senses can stir a reader's soul as in the Song of Songs 2:1-7:

Beloved

1 I am a rose of Sharon, a lily of the valleys.

Lover

2 Like a lily among thorns is my darling among the maidens.

Beloved

3 Like an apple tree among the trees of the forest is my lover among the young
men. I delight to sit in his shade, and his fruit is sweet to my taste. 4 He has taken
me to the banquet hall, and his banner over me is love. 5 Strengthen me with
raisins, refresh me with apples, for I am faint with love. 6 His left arm is under my
head, and his right arm embraces me.

7 Daughters of Jerusalem, I charge you by the gazelles and by the does of the field: Do not arouse or awaken love until it so desires.

ANALYSIS QUESTIONS

8. The writer might have said his ministers are "dynamic" but instead says they are "a flame of fire." Is this a metaphor, or are they actually flames? No matter which interpretation you choose, what sensory impressions did you experience due to the "flame" language? Which style of saying it do you like better? Why?

---

9. Write a few sentences describing the image that jumped into your mind when you read the metaphor predicting that the heavens "will all grow old like a garment."

10. Write a one paragraph summary of Song of Songs 2:1-7 in your own words.

WRITING ASSIGNMENT

1. It is time to write your own description on a topic related to the one you used when writing the narrative. In fact, your instructor might give you the option of adding a page worth of description to your previous narrative. If so, highlight or underline the added material so it is clear to the reader that descriptive elements have been added.

2. Description presents impressions. **Assignment:** Use all five senses (taste, touch, smell, sight, sound) in your writing to convey the same sensory impressions for the reader as you experienced when you became passionate about the subject.

3. Adjectives and adverbs add interesting description. (She walked *carefully* over the *slippery* ice). **Assignment:** Without overdoing it, experiment with using carefully chosen adjectives and adverbs in every paragraph.

4. Write your one-page description. Try to capture the sensations that make your topic fascinating. Express yourself with all five senses: taste, touch, smell, sight, and sound. Make your listener want to love and experience this topic as much as you do.

5. Bring your description to class when it is due for peer-review by a classmate.

(name of person writing review) ____________________________________

PEER REVIEW: It is time to have a fellow student read and evaluate the description paper. The instructor is likely to assign partners for students who have just done the same exercise.

____ The entire description must be written from the third-person point of view. Circle all the words like "I," "we," and "you" and make suggestions to help the writer get it all in third person.

____ Sniff through the description again, this time looking for evidence that all five senses are used. Whenever you detect "taste," "touch," "smell," "sight," or "sound," write that word in the margin. Make sure all five senses are used to their full effect.

____ Review the use of <u>adjectives</u>—*clever* describing words that modify nouns—to make sure they are used effectively. Suggest additional adjectives that might strengthen the paper.

____ Review the use of <u>adverbs</u>—words that *cleverly* alter the meaning of verbs—to make sure they are used effectively. Suggest additional adverbs that might strengthen the paper.

____ Underline the <u>verbs</u> in key sentences and contemplate stronger words to portray the same action. Be suspicious of any sentence beginning with "there are" or "it is" as well as excessive use of the word "that." These sentences call for stronger verbs or more precise subjects.

____ How do you *feel* after reading this description? Have you lost yourself in the description—have you been transported into another world? If not, have you at least caught the author's enthusiasm? If so, what "grabbed" you and effectively communicated this enthusiasm? If not, what suggestions can you give to make it grab you? Write your suggestions on the back of the student's paper.

____ Review the paper one last time for correct spelling and punctuation. For guidelines, see the *MLA Handbook* 3.1 (spelling) and 3.2 (punctuation). To get some idea of the importance of punctuation, consider which punctuation you agree with in the following sentence:

> "A woman, without her man, is nothing."
>
> "A woman: without her, man is nothing" (Truss 13).

Research Time

____ Where should more facts be added to give this paper more credibility?

____ Suggest a source where this author might look up more information that would strengthen the content of this paper.

____ Write a few reasons why this paper would be better if it had the facts and information suggested in the above questions.

PLANNING THE REWRITE

In addition to carefully considering the suggestions of the peer reviewer, read the *MLA Handbook* 3.1-3.8 "The Mechanics of Writing" and 1.9 "Writing Drafts" for helpful rewriting suggestions. As with the narrative assignment, the final draft of the description should be written on computer and formatted like the sample in the *MLA Handbook* page 117 with header, margins, title, double spacing, and other details exactly as modeled.

LITERATURE REVIEW

Add reliable details to your description following these guidelines: Go to the library catalog and locate a book on your topic. Find the book in your library and write down at least one subject heading from the book:

Subject heading ____

Now fill in the information requested below:

Author: ____

Title of book: ____

City of publisher: ____

Name of publisher: ____

Date of publication: ____

Is there a bibliography at the end of the book? ____ yes ____ no

In the space below, speculate on the potential advantages of reading books in your subject area from highly reputable publishers that also contain a bibliography:

____

____

____

____

Just as you did on the narrative paper, write a literature review by preparing a paraphrase, summary, and quote from this new source:

1. **Paraphrase** an important section of the book. Be careful to avoid plagiarism as explained in the *MLA Handbook* 2.5.
2. **Summarize** several pages of the book in your own words.
3. **Quote** one excellent example of descriptive writing by copying it carefully into your paper. Put quote marks around the material and insert an appropriate introduction such as, Blanchard writes, "Never eat olives after midnight or you'll get cramps."

To find out what information to put in a Works Cited page to accompany the above paraphrase, summary, and quote, look up "books" in the index of the *MLA Handbook* (page 268). The index entries will refer you to other sections of the *MLA Handbook*. When you find the correct format to follow, write that information in your paper *in the correct format*.

PARENTHETICAL REFERENCE

Look in the *MLA* index to find the entry concerning "books . . . in parenthetical references" to find out how to reference your quote. Insert the parenthetical reference at the end of the above paraphrase, summary, and quote *in the correct format*. Insert the new information from this worksheet into the appropriate places in the final draft of the description.

Guidelines on how to gracefully integrate the new research with the paper you have written are provided in chapter six of the *MLA Handbook*. Pay particular attention to section 6.3 beginning on page 216. In addition to those instructions, be sure to create a context that shows the reader precisely how this new material is an integral part of your paper.

Include a Works Cited page with your paper. The format should use double spacing, hanging indentation, alphabetical order, and look exactly like the Works Cited page at the end of this book, or the samples on page 232 of the *MLA Handbook.*

Tip One: How to use subject pronouns

Academic writing generally favors third person. However, when first person is used, remember that the subject pronouns *I, he, she, it, you, they,* and *we* are always used as subjects. The object pronouns *him, her, me, them,* and *us* are never used as subjects. When a pronoun is part of a compound subject, treat it as the only subject when deciding what pronoun to use. For example, students confused by whether to use *I* or *me* with compound subjects can learn from these examples: "I like pizza." Therefore, "My wife and I like pizza." "The pizza belongs to me"(not "I"). Therefore, "The pizza belongs to my wife and me" (not "I").

Tip Two: When to capitalize proper pronouns

If you can insert the person's name, capitalize the substituted word: "I said Dad was tall." If you cannot insert the person's name, do not capitalize: "I said my dad was tall."

CHAPTER 3: PROCESS

Narrative writing tells a story; descriptive writing adds pizzazz. Another important step is to identify and explain a **process** in a chosen academic discipline. All disciplines follow some sort of **process**. Both medical doctors and auto mechanics perform a *diagnosis* by following an established *process* to decide what is wrong with people and vehicles. Composers have a set of rules to follow when writing each particular variety of music. When Johann Sebastian Bach wrote his *Fugue in G. Minor*, he followed the prescribed pattern for a fugue by starting out with a theme that repeats throughout the composition in different voices (Bach). He knew voices can overlap and invert, and be played backward or repeated.

Process papers explain how a thing happened, or how it can be made to happen. Articles about processes make up the bulk of many professional journals, and one objective of this chapter is to introduce students to the periodical publications in their discipline, and to encourage them to make it a habit to read those magazines and journals.

PROCESS MODELS

Process is an ancient form of writing and appears in a document attributed to Moses:

> Now the earth was corrupt in God's sight, and the earth was filled with violence. And God saw the earth, and behold, it was corrupt; for all flesh had corrupted their way upon the earth. And God said to Noah, "I have determined to make an end of all flesh; for the earth is filled with violence through them; behold, I will destroy them with the earth. Make yourself an ark of gopher wood; make rooms

> in the ark, and cover it inside and out with pitch. This is how you are to make it: the length of the ark three hundred cubits, its breadth fifty cubits, and its height thirty cubits. Make a roof for the ark, and finish it to a cubit above; and set the door of the ark in its side; make it with lower, second, and third decks. For behold, I will bring a flood of waters upon the earth, to destroy all flesh in which is the breath of life from under heaven; everything that is on the earth shall die. But I will establish my covenant with you; and you shall come into the ark, you, your sons, your wife, and your sons' wives with you. And of every living thing of all flesh, you shall bring two of every sort into the ark, to keep them alive with you; they shall be male and female. Of the birds according to their kinds, and of the animals according to their kinds, of every creeping thing of the ground according to its kind, two of every sort shall come in to you, to keep them alive. Also take with you every sort of food that is eaten, and store it up; and it shall serve as food for you and for them." Noah did this; he did all that God commanded him. (Gen. 6:11-22, RSV)

ANALYSIS QUESTIONS

1. What is God's purpose for the ark based on the process he outlined for Noah?
2. What size and shape should the ark be, and what materials should be used to build it?
3. What will Noah do with the ark when he has finished building it?
4. What questions might Noah have that are not answered by the instructions?

Equally detailed instructions on how to follow a carefully prescribed process are given in 2 Chronicles 2 when Solomon sets out to build the temple, but process instructions are not limited to merely outlining how to do something. The technique is employed in Revelation 21:9-

27 in reference to “the Bride, the wife of the Lamb" (Rev. 21:9) depicted as “the holy city Jerusalem coming down out of heaven from God" (Rev. 21:10).

THE SCIENTIFIC METHOD[1]

Process is most obvious in scientific pursuits. Francis Bacon (1561-1626) developed the Scientific Method, a process for doing research and verifying a hypothesis by following six logical steps:

1. Observation: Learning about any event noted through the senses.
   a. must be documented scientifically
   b. must be repeatable under similar conditions
   c. must be objective (factual)
2. Problem: A question asked about an observation.
   a. must contain only one unknown
   b. must use testable question words that point to a concrete answer
3. Hypothesis: One possible answer to the problem question.
   a. must answer question in a testable fashion
   b. must be limited to one established factor
   c. must include a reason
   bd usually requires research in order to make an "educated" guess
4. Experiment: A test designed to prove or disprove the hypothesis.
   a. must be controlled
   b. must have only one variable
   c. must collect measurable data or information
5. Data Analysis: Data collected must be interpreted based on the hypothesis.

---

[1] Chapter 11 discusses the Scientific Method as a form of inductive logic.

a. raw data must be organized into a readable form (charts, graphs, etc.)

b. data must show the relationship between the experiment and the question

6. Conclusion: A Statement that compares the hypothesis to the data.

a. must use data to state the correctness of the hypothesis, which will turn out to be either right or wrong

b. If the hypothesis is correct, it should be able to be replicated to validate results

c. If the hypothesis is incorrect or unanswered, then

i. the experiment must be re-designed, or

ii. the question or hypothesis must be restated.

DISCOURSE COMMUNITIES

Process papers launch researchers into the technical jargon of the discourse community in which they work. Theologians have their own language set. So do psychologists, computer programmers, biologists, auto mechanics, physicians, and hundreds of other discourse communities. Such individuals are permitted to write in the first person plural ("we" and "our") when they speak for a clearly defined group of specialists. A letter from an undergraduate physics major illustrates permitted usage when writing about a process:

> One theory states that in the nucleus of Helium-3 and He-4, the two protons might be combined in a pre-existing delta particle with +2 charge. We know Δ particles exist, but they're hard to find in the nucleus because first they must be gotten OUT of the nucleus, and once outside they tend to decay into two protons. The experiment was carried out at the Los Alamos National Laboratory Neutron Science Center (LANSCE). LANSCE houses a proton beam in the Linear Accelerator (LINAC) in which the p+s are accelerated to a significant

> fraction of the speed of light (186,282.4 miles per second). They then collide with a tungsten spallation target, which ejects neutrons and protons. The facility provides several collimators for multiple neutron beam paths for different research groups. We use Building 34 to set up a pressurized tank of either He-3 or He-4 with plastic scintillators coupled with photomultiplier tubes at 45° angles to the neutron beam and on the other side of the He target tank. Based on the energies of the protons, we determine if at least some of the protons decayed from Δ++. (Runyon)

ISAAC NEWTON (1642-1727)

Sixteen years after Francis Bacon died, Isaac Newton was born. He put the Scientific Method to excellent use. Famous for identifying the universal law of gravity, he also invented machines, made discoveries in optics and mathematics, designed the first reflecting telescope, and revolutionized the study of mechanics and physics. Newton's letter to the Royal Society concerning his theory about light and colors illustrates how describing a process enhances the reader's understanding, and if it is well done, the reader can replicate the process:

> In the beginning of the year 1666 (at which time I applied myself to the grinding of optic glasses of other figures than spherical) I procured me a triangular glass prism to try therewith the celebrated phenomena of colors. And in order thereto having darkened my chamber and made a small hole in my window-shuts to let in a convenient quantity of the sun's light, I placed my prism at his entrance that it might be thereby refracted to the opposite wall. It was at first a very pleasing divertissement to view the vivid and intense colors produced thereby; but after a while, applying myself to consider them more circumspectly, I became surprised

> to see them in an *oblong* form, which according to the received laws of refraction I expected should have been *circular*. (2156)

The full process Newton followed with this experiment takes many pages to complete, but this sample paragraph illustrates the value to a student in almost any discipline of cultivating the ability to write a process paper.

THE LORAX

Process is not limited to giving instructions or explaining scientific concepts. It is also used in prose and poetry, fact and fiction—whenever an author wishes to provide information in chronological order. Many short stories are fundamentally process papers that incorporate narrative and descriptive writing. A few excerpts from *The Lorax* by Dr. Seuss illustrate this point. Phrases that are primarily process in nature are underlined:

> Way back in the days when the grass was still green
> and the pond was still wet and the clouds were still clean,
> and the song of the Swomee-Swans rang out in space. . . .
> one morning, I came to this glorious place.
> And I first saw the trees! The Truffula Trees!
> . . . Mile after mile in the fresh morning breeze. . . .
> I felt a great leaping of joy in my heart.
> I knew just what I'd do! I unloaded my cart.
> In no time at all, I had built a small shop.
> Then I chopped down a Truffula Tree with one chop.
> And with great skillful skill and with great speedy speed,
> I took the soft tuft. And I knitted a thneed!

Now he gets lectured by the Lorax for his environmental abuse, but just as the Lorax says, "Sir! You are crazy with greed. There is no one on earth who would buy that fool Thneed," he manages to sell one and then hatches a plan to make more:

> I rushed 'cross the room, and in no time at all,
> built a radio-phone. *I put in a quick call*.
> I called all my brothers and uncles and aunts
> and I said, "Listen here! Here's a wonderful chance
> for the whole Once-ler Family to get mighty rich!
> Get over here fast! Take the road to North Nitch.
> Turn left at Weehawken. Sharp right at South Stitch."
> … Now, chopping one tree at a time was too slow.
> So I quickly invented my Super-Axe-Hacker
> which whacked off four Truffula Trees at one smacker.
> We were making Thneeds four times as fast as before. . . .
> I biggered my factory. I biggered my roads.
> I biggered my wagons. I biggered the loads
> of the thneeds I shipped out. . . .
> "What's *more*," snapped the Lorax. (His dander was up.)
> "Let me say a few words about Gluppity-Glupp.
> Your machinery chugs on, day and night without stop
> Making Gluppity-Glupp. Also Schloppity-Schlopp.
> And what do you do with this leftover goo?
> . . ."You're glumping the pond where the Humming-Fish hummed!
> No more can they hum, for their gills are all gummed.

So I'm sending them off. Oh, their future is dreary."

[Earlier printings add, "I hear things are just as bad up in Lake Erie."]

WRITING ASSIGNMENT

The first step in creating a process paper is to imagine the possible processes common in your discipline, followed by research into what has already been done by specialists in the given field of study. You can then write a paper analyzing a process already carried out by others, or you can create your own process based on models provided by others.

1. Identify your topic here—some aspect of the same topic as your narrative and description papers: English Writing
2. Write a page of notes to yourself identifying a process integral to your topic. As you brainstorm the potential intricacies, don't just write, "The artist must stretch her canvas and mix her paints before creating an oil painting." That is a little too obvious. A better approach is to identify the process by which she knows how to create a palette of visual effects by mixing primary colors.
3. Now that you have brainstormed a process appropriate to your discourse community, do research to find out the processes explained by specialists in your field of study. These usually appear in scholarly journals and can be located using the following steps on a computer at your college or university library:

A: Select a **FirstSearch** database such as WilsonSelectPlus by using the "Jump to Advanced Search" option. Find an article in a professional journal on your topic and save it on your computer or print appropriate pages for future reference.

B: **Paraphrase, summarize, and quote** material from this source just as you did in the **literature reviews** as explained in Chapters 1 and 2. If you cite an electronic full-text article from a database such as WilsonSelectPlus, MLA requires that the citation include the elements shown here (see *MLA Handbook* 181-184):

Wise, Charles R. "Organizing for Homeland Security." Public Administration Review 62 (2002): 131-144. WilsonSelectPlus [specific database]. FirstSearch [database provider]. SAU Library [library name]. Web. 25 Aug. 2009 [date viewed/printed].

C: Now select an **InfoTrac** database and find an article on your topic. Save it on your computer or print appropriate pages for future reference.

D: **Paraphrase, summarize, and quote** material from these sources just as you did in FirstSearch, following *MLA Handbook* guidelines for documentation.

E: Write the process paper on computer with correct MLA documentation and formatting. This will give the peer reviewer opportunity to help you detect documentation errors in addition to the usual mistakes which must be corrected before turning in the process paper for a grade.

(name of person writing review) ____________________________________

PEER REVIEW: A fellow student should read and evaluate the process paper. The instructor is likely to assign partners for students who have just done the same exercise.

____ Evaluate the point of view. Is it appropriate for the process being analyzed? It must be written from the third-person point of view unless the author represents a discourse community. In this case, first person plural may be used: ("We discovered," "Our research indicates").

Note: *Implied* second person may be used if instructions are being given, as in "set the temperature at 360," "pour the mixture slowly into the beaker."

Pick one: a. ____ The audience is someone who will perform the process.

b. ____ The audience will merely understand the process.

____ Make sure the writer has used clear and unambiguous language so the reader will not encounter unnecessary frustration and inconvenience.

____ Confirm that all requirements such as time and supplies needed are clearly indicated.

____ Evaluate the effectiveness of warnings to readers about any possible harm in carrying out this process.

____ Make sure instructions or steps are given in a logical and appropriate order. If necessary, suggest a revised structure and move paragraphs as needed.

____ Confirm that each paragraph has only one central idea.

____ Delete any unnecessary details.

____ Be sure that the connections between sentences and paragraphs are effective.

____ Make sure the Works Cited are formatted accurately based on section 5.6 of the *MLA Handbook.*

____ List any questions the author has failed to answer.

PLANNING THE REWRITE

In addition to carefully considering the suggestions of the peer reviewer, review the *MLA Handbook* 3.1-3.8 "The Mechanics of Writing" and 1.9 "Writing Drafts" for helpful rewriting suggestions. Rewrite the process paper into a logical, smooth-flowing set of instructions that anyone who knows the language of your discourse community can follow.

Thought to ponder: This chapter is itself a process paper from a discourse community explaining how to write a paper in acceptable MLA format. Write a list of the new vocabulary words you have gained from your exposure to this process:

____

____

____

____

____

____

____

____

CHAPTER 4: DEFINITION

Narrative tells a story, description adds interest, and process explains how a thing is done. A fourth form of academic writing involves **definition.** *Simple* definitions appear in dictionaries and can be formulated at very primitive levels. "Sterile" can mean "infertile, barren, incapable of producing offspring," or "mentally or spiritually barren," or "free from micro-organisms, aseptic" (OED).

Simple definitions provide a starting point for extended definitions. For example, the dictionary defines "love" as "that state of feeling with regard to a person which manifests itself in concern for the person's welfare" (OED). But even children can quickly get beyond that when asked what love means. Karl, age five, put it in the dating context: "Love is when a girl puts on perfume and a boy puts on shaving cologne and they go out and smell each other." Noelle said, "Love is when you tell a guy you like his shirt—then he wears it every day." Karen added, "When you love somebody, your eyelashes go up and down and little stars come out of you."

More theologically sophisticated children observed, "Love is what's in the room with you at Christmas if you stop opening presents and listen." Nikka, age six, suggested, "If you want to learn to love better, you should start with a friend who you hate." Jessica advised, "You shouldn't say, 'I love you,' unless you mean it. But if you mean it, say it a lot. People forget."

Other youngsters used illustrations to explain love. Rebecca, age eight, said, "When my grandmother got arthritis, she couldn't bend over and paint her toenails, so my grandfather does it for her, even when his hands got arthritis, too. That's Love." Billy, age four, said it this way:

"When someone loves you, the way they say your name is different. You just know that your name is safe in their mouth." Four-year-old Lauren said, "I know my older sister loves me because she gives me all her old clothes and has to go out and buy new ones."

The above comments by children are extensions on the definition of love. **Extended definitions** explain an abstract concept in more detail to give readers sophisticated insight. Consider the word "ecclesiology," a Greek-derived word referring to the Church. A book exploring the meaning of this term argues that while "The Council of Nicea declared that the church is *one, holy, catholic*, and *apostolic*," the New Testament reveals that "it would be more biblically accurate to say that the church is:

DIVERSE as well as ONE

CHARISMATIC as well as HOLY

LOCAL as well as CATHOLIC or UNIVERSAL

PROPHETIC as well as APOSTOLIC." (Snyder and Runyon 17, 22)

These authors wrote an entire book to help define for Christians a more accurate understanding of "ecclesiology." College students in every discipline should begin reading such publications as they learn the language of their discourse community and write their own extended definitions.

DEFINITION MODEL

The Apostle Paul's famous "love" chapter in his letter to the Corinthians is an extended definition. Corinth at the time of his writing was the "love" capital of the world. This trading city located on the isthmus between the Aegean and Ionian seas teamed with people who equated love with sex thanks to the temple of Poseidon, a place "given over to the worship of the Corinthian Aphrodite (probably a counterpart of the Syrian Astarte) whose temple on the Acrocorinth had more than 1,000 *hierodouloi* (female prostitutes)" (Gaebelein 176). Paul introduces a new definition of love that would have astounded the Corinthian audience.

Extended Definition of Love: 1 Corinthians 13 (American Standard Version)

[1]If I speak with the tongues of men and of angels, but have not love, I am become sounding
brass, or a clanging cymbal. [2]And if I have *the gift of* prophecy, and know all mysteries and all
knowledge; and if I have all faith, so as to remove mountains, but have not love, I am nothing.
[3]And if I bestow all my goods to feed *the poor*, and if I give my body to be burned, but have not
love, it profiteth me nothing. [4]Love suffereth long, *and* is kind; love envieth not; love vaunteth
not itself, is not puffed up, [5]doth not behave itself unseemly, seeketh not its own, is not
provoked, taketh not account of evil; [6]rejoiceth not in unrighteousness, but rejoiceth with the
truth; [7]beareth all things, believeth all things, hopeth all things, endureth all things. [8]Love never
faileth: but whether *there be* prophecies, they shall be done away; whether *there be* tongues, they
shall cease; whether *there be* knowledge, it shall be done away. [9]For we know in part, and we
prophesy in part; [10]but when that which is perfect is come, that which is in part shall be done
away. [11]When I was a child, I spake as a child, I felt as a child, I thought as a child: now that I
am become a man, I have put away childish things. [12]For now we see in a mirror, darkly; but
then face to face: now I know in part; but then shall I know fully even as also I was fully known.
[13]But now abideth faith, hope, love, these three; and the greatest of these is love.

ANALYSIS QUESTIONS

1. Make a list of the synonyms Paul used to make his new definition of love more easily understood. (A synonym is an equivalent word, or a word or phrase having the same general sense as another word in the same language.)
2. Distinguish between the "simple" definitions and the "extended" definitions in this essay.
3. Write a paragraph about any new insights you gained about the topic of "love" from having read this definition.

WRITING ASSIGNMENT

Now it is time to write an extended definition. Begin by recognizing that entire books have been written to define a word or concept. Locate a book specific to the topic you are writing about for your extended definition paper. **Hint:** The bibliographies or Works Cited pages of publications consulted for earlier papers are a good place to begin.

1. When you find a book, look in the table of the contents for a section closely related to your area of interest and write a literature review on that section (see guidelines in chapters one and two). Your literature review should summarize, paraphrase, and quote as necessary to capture the essence of the source you are using.
2. Look at pages 214-219 of the *MLA Handbook* to find out what information to put in a parenthetical reference to identify the above source.
3. Look at pages 129-135 of your *MLA Handbook* to find out what information to put in a Works Cited to accompany the material from the above book, and write it down in the correct format.

Source one: ____

4. Follow this same format for additional sources.

Source two: ____

Source three: ____

Be sure to list all sources in your Works Cited page, and format each source according to guidelines given in the *MLA Handbook* (129-212).

(name of person writing review) ____

PEER REVIEW: Have a fellow student read and evaluate the extended definition paper. The instructor is likely to assign partners for students who have just done the same exercise.

1. Read the introduction paragraph and the conclusion paragraph. Edit as necessary so they would belong together if the rest of the paper were missing.

2. Cross out all first person (I, me, my, we, us, our) and all second person (you, your) words to help the author convert the entire manuscript to third person.

3. Consider these questions:

____ Are the purpose and audience clear and appropriate?

____ Does the paper avoid the common pitfalls of overly broad, or overly narrow definition?

____ Are the methods of development suitable for the topic?

____ Is the paper organized effectively? That is, does it flow logically and answer questions in the order the reader is likely to ask them?

____ Identify the most boring part and make suggestions on how to make it more interesting.

____ Review for accuracy the MLA format, punctuation and grammar, and parenthetical references and Works Cited.

____ Read aloud the portions of the definition that immediately precede and follow source material that is summarized, paraphrased, or quoted. (Parenthetical documentation should follow every instance.) Correct the writing style as necessary so the researched material flows smoothly with the author's voice.

____ Make suggestions on how the researched material can be more fully integrated into the paper in a way that reflects the author's analysis and synthesis of the research.

PLANNING THE REWRITE

Carefully consider the suggestions of the peer reviewer as you rewrite the extended definition in such a logical and clear way that a person previously unfamiliar with the term being defined will understand. Also, be certain that the format and structure of all parenthetical references and Works Cited entries are precisely correct according to the *MLA Handbook.* Finally, be absolutely certain that your extended definition in no way plagiarizes the original sources. Instructions on how to avoid plagiarism are provided in the *MLA Handbook.*

PLAGIARISM QUIZ

Find the answers to the questions below on pages 51-61 of the *MLA Handbook.*

	T	F	
1.	____	F	*Plagiarism* derives from the Greek word *plagias* ("plate thief").
2.	T	____	Unacknowledged use of ideas, information, or expressions is intellectual theft.
3.	T	____	Passing off another person's material as your own constitutes fraud.
4.	____	F	Copyright rules limit plagiarism to a legal offense with no ethical implications.
5.	____	F	Plagiarists easily recover the trust of those they try to deceive.
6.	T	____	Careful documentation tends to discourage the circulation of error.
7.	____	F	Plagiarism is impossible to avoid when using electronic or web publications.
8.	T	____	Because research has the power to affect opinions and actions, responsible writers compose their work with great care, often spending as much time documenting sources as writing original material.

(quiz continues on next page)

Multiple Choice

9. Regarding unintentional plagiarism, the *MLA Handbook* suggests that writers should keep careful notes on

a. their ideas

b. their summaries and paraphrases of the ideas and facts of others

c. exact wording copied from sources

d. all of the above

e. none of the above

10. Documentation is not needed in the following instances. (Circle all that apply.)

a. When quoting familiar proverbs or well-known quotations.

b. When writing statements of common knowledge.

c. When quoting the Bible or other well-known religious documents.

d. When quoting daily newspapers or websites with no print equivalent.

e. When quoting information obtained by personal interviews or survey research.

The importance of avoiding plagiarism cannot be overstated. Some university professors (including the author of this text) automatically fail any student caught plagiarizing, and many educational institutions publish their own plagiarism guidelines which they expect students to know and follow. For more information, an internet search on "plagiarism" will turn up numerous sources and guidelines for learning how to avoid plagiarism.

CHAPTER 5: ILLUSTRATION

All the forms of writing covered so far in this text, narrative, description, process, and definition can be improved with **illustrations.** Some definitions of love in the last chapter used illustrations, which can be as brief as a few words or as long as a chapter. When five-year-old Karl tried to define love he actually illustrated it: "Love is when a girl puts on perfume and a boy puts on shaving cologne and they go out and smell each other."

Illustration is the art of comparing a new concept with something already familiar to the reader, and illustrations are chosen based on the audience. A psychologist talking to a computer technician illustrates his point successfully when he says that the brain stores information "like a silicon chip." The same message needs to be illustrated differently to children in the African bush where there is no electricity or computers. Perhaps the psychologist will make some reference to an elephant if he is aware of the saying in Africa that "elephants never forget."

In literature, culturally relevant symbols are often used to convey meaning. The symbol often dictates the interpretation. A father who learns to tell time with an analogue watch might envision time as passing in a “clock-wise” direction—in a circle to the right. He may extrapolate from this image of minutes and hours a mental picture of the calendar as a circle with March in the three o’clock position, June at six o’clock, September at nine o’clock, and the break between December and January at precisely midnight. If this man’s son learns to tell time via a digital watch and therefore envisions days, months, and years as lined up in linear fashion from left to right, he represents a paradigm shift—the two types of clocks have become opposing symbols that influence the way time is perceived. Due to this shift, the son may not understand his father's "clockwise" symbol.

Illustration is a high art. It must always serve the larger context. The risk is that the illustration will overtake the message. Many a pastor has thought he preached on "The Consequences of Disobedience" when most people in attendance missed his point and thought he just told a story about a big fish that swallowed Jonah. Successful illustrations clarify the point or help readers understand a concept in deeper ways.

ILLUSTRATION MODELS

When the reader has no possible reference point for understanding the thing being taught, an illustration may be the only way to explain a concept. God has this problem—without revelation, earth-bound humankind has no way to comprehend heaven-grounded truth. Therefore, it is no surprise that the Bible provides some of the finest models of the art of illustration. Three selections are provided below.

James 2 (New Century Version)

1 My dear brothers and sisters, as believers in our glorious Lord Jesus Christ, never think
some people are more important than others. 2 Suppose someone comes into your church meeting
wearing nice clothes and a gold ring. At the same time a poor person comes in wearing old, dirty
clothes. 3 You show special attention to the one wearing nice clothes and say, “Please, sit here in
this good seat.” But you say to the poor person, “Stand over there,” or, “Sit on the floor by my
feet.” 4 What are you doing? You are making some people more important than others, and with
evil thoughts you are deciding that one person is better.

5 Listen, my dear brothers and sisters! God chose the poor in the world to be rich with faith
and to receive the kingdom God promised to those who love him. 6 But you show no respect to

the poor. The rich are always trying to control your lives. They are the ones who take you to
court. 7 And they are the ones who speak against Jesus, who owns you.

8 This royal law is found in the Scriptures: "Love your neighbor as you love yourself." If you
obey this law, you are doing right. 9 But if you treat one person as being more important than
another, you are sinning. You are guilty of breaking God's law. 10 A person who follows all of
God's law but fails to obey even one command is guilty of breaking all the commands in that
law. 11 The same God who said, "You must not be guilty of adultery," also said, "You must not
murder anyone." So if you do not take part in adultery but you murder someone, you are guilty
of breaking all of God's law. 12 In everything you say and do, remember that you will be judged
by the law that makes people free. 13 So you must show mercy to others, or God will not show
mercy to you when he judges you. But the person who shows mercy can stand without fear at the
judgement.

Faith and Good Works

14 My brothers and sisters, if people say they have faith, but do nothing, their faith is worth
nothing. Can faith like that save them? 15 A brother or sister in Christ might need clothes or food.
16 If you say to that person, "God be with you! I hope you stay warm and get plenty to eat," but
you do not give what that person needs, your words are worth nothing. 17 In the same way, faith
that is alone—that does nothing—is dead.

18 Someone might say, "You have faith, but I have deeds." Show me your faith without doing
anything, and I will show you my faith by what I do. 19 You believe there is one God. Good! But
the demons believe that, too, and they tremble with fear.

20 You foolish person! Must you be shown that faith that does nothing is worth nothing?
21 Abraham, our ancestor, was made right with God by what he did when he offered his son Isaac

on the altar. 22 So you see that Abraham's faith and the things he did worked together. His faith
was made perfect by what he did. 23 This shows the full meaning of the Scripture that says:
"Abraham believed God, and God accepted Abraham's faith, and that faith made him right with
God." And Abraham was called God's friend. 24 So you see that people are made right with God
by what they do, not by faith only.

25 Another example is Rahab, a prostitute, who was made right with God by something she
did. She welcomed the spies into her home and helped them escape by a different road.
26 Just as a person's body that does not have a spirit is dead, so faith that does nothing is dead!

ANALYSIS QUESTIONS

1. List all of the examples used by the author to illustrate his point.
2. How does each example make the above comments by James more interesting and easy to understand?

I Corinthians 12 (The Message)

What I want to talk about now is the various ways God's Spirit gets worked into our lives. This is complex and often misunderstood, but I want you to be informed and knowledgeable. Remember how you were when you didn't know God, led from one phony god to another, never knowing what you were doing, just doing it because everybody else did it? It's different in this life. God wants us to use our intelligence, to seek to understand as well as we can. For instance, by using your heads, you know perfectly well that the Spirit of God would never prompt anyone to say "Jesus be damned!" Nor would anyone be inclined to say "Jesus is Master!" without the insight of the Holy Spirit.

God's various gifts are handed out everywhere; but they all originate in God's Spirit. God's various ministries are carried out everywhere; but they all originate in God's Spirit. God's various expressions of power are in action everywhere; but God himself is behind it all. Each person is given something to do that shows who God is: Everyone gets in on it, everyone benefits. All kinds of things are handed out by the Spirit, and to all kinds of people! The variety is wonderful: wise counsel, clear understanding, simple trust, healing the sick, miraculous acts, proclamation, distinguishing between spirits, tongues, interpretation of tongues. All these gifts have a common origin, but are handed out one by one by the one Spirit of God. He decides who gets what, and when.

You can easily enough see how this kind of thing works by looking no further than your own body. Your body has many parts—limbs, organs, cells—but no matter how many parts you can name, you're still one body. It's exactly the same with Christ. By means of his one Spirit, we all said goodbye to our partial and piecemeal lives. We each used to independently call our own shots, but then we entered into a large and integrated life in which he has the final say in everything. (This is what we proclaimed in word and action when we were baptized.) Each of us is now a part of his resurrection body, refreshed and sustained at one fountain—his Spirit—where we all come to drink. The old labels we once used to identify ourselves—labels like Jew or Greek, slave or free—are no longer useful. We need something larger, more comprehensive.

I want you to think about how all this makes you more significant, not less. A body isn't just a single part blown up into something huge. It's all the different-but-similar parts arranged and functioning together. If Foot said, "I'm not elegant like Hand, embellished with rings; I guess I don't belong to this body," would that make it so? If Ear said, "I'm not beautiful like Eye, limpid and expressive; I don't deserve a place on the head," would you want to remove it from the body? If the body was all eye, how could it hear? If all ear, how could it smell? As it is, we see that God has carefully placed each part of the body right where he wanted it.

But I also want you to think about how this keeps your significance from getting blown up into self-importance. For no matter how significant you are, it is only because of what you are a part of. An enormous eye or a gigantic hand wouldn't be a body, but a monster. What we have is one body with many parts, each its proper size and in its proper place. No part is important on its own. Can you imagine Eye telling Hand, "Get lost; I don't need you"? Or, Head telling Foot, "You're fired; your job has been phased out"? As a matter of fact, in practice it works the other way—the "lower" the part, the more basic, and therefore necessary. You can live without an eye, for instance, but not without a stomach. When it's a part of your own body you are concerned with, it makes no difference whether the part is visible or clothed, higher or lower. You give it dignity and honor just as it is, without comparisons. If anything, you have more concern for the lower parts than the higher. If you had to choose, wouldn't you prefer good digestion to full-bodied hair?

The way God designed our bodies is a model for understanding our lives together as a church: every part dependent on every other part, the parts we mention and the parts we don't, the parts we see and the parts we don't. If one part hurts, every other part is involved in the hurt, and in the healing. If one part flourishes, every other part enters into the exuberance.

You are Christ's body—that's who you are! You must never forget this. Only as you accept your part of that body does your "part" mean anything. You're familiar with some of the parts that God has formed in his church, which is his "body": apostles, prophets, teachers, miracle, workers, healers, helpers, organizers, those who pray in tongues. But it's obvious by now, isn't it, that Christ's church is a complete Body and not a gigantic, unidimensional Part? It's not all Apostle, not all Prophet, not all Miracle Worker, not all Healer, not all Prayer in Tongues, not all Interpreter of Tongues. And yet some of you keep competing for so-called "important" parts. But now I want to lay out a far better way for you.

ANALYSIS QUESTIONS

3. Metaphors are a type of illustration. (See Chapter 2 for more information on metaphors.) How does the extended metaphor of the "Body" help the reader comprehend the author's meaning?
4. Describe the images that jump into your mind as you read about the "Body" metaphor.
5. Try to think of another metaphor that could illustrate the same truth to a modern reader. Is your metaphor better than Paul's? Why or why not?
6. How does the author's sense of humor contribute to make the passage more interesting and enjoyable to read?

Matthew 20 (New International Version)

1 "For the kingdom of heaven is like a landowner who went out early in the morning to hire
men to work in his vineyard. 2 He agreed to pay them a denarius for the day and sent them into
his vineyard.

3 "About the third hour he went out and saw others standing in the marketplace doing nothing.
4 He told them, 'You also go and work in my vineyard, and I will pay you whatever is right.' 5 So
they went.

"He went out again about the sixth hour and the ninth hour and did the same thing. 6 About
the eleventh hour he went out and found still others standing around. He asked them, 'Why have
you been standing here all day long doing nothing?'

7 "'Because no one has hired us,' they answered.

"He said to them, 'You also go and work in my vineyard.'

8 "When evening came, the owner of the vineyard said to his foreman, 'Call the workers and
pay them their wages, beginning with the last ones hired and going on to the first.'

[9]"The workers who were hired about the eleventh hour came and each received a denarius.
[10]So when those came who were hired first, they expected to receive more. But each one of them
also received a denarius. [11]When they received it, they began to grumble against the landowner.
[12]'These men who were hired last worked only one hour,' they said, 'and you have made them
equal to us who have borne the burden of the work and the heat of the day.'

[13]"But he answered one of them, 'Friend, I am not being unfair to you. Didn't you agree to
work for a denarius? [14]Take your pay and go. I want to give the man who was hired last the same
as I gave you. [15]Don't I have the right to do what I want with my own money? Or are you
envious because I am generous?'

[16]"So the last will be first, and the first will be last."

ANALYSIS QUESTIONS

7. Jesus was a master at telling stories to illustrate difficult concepts. What do you understand about heaven now that was not clear to you before reading this?
8. How did the illustrations of Jesus help you gain these new insights?
9. What have you learned from this story about God's point of view?

WRITING ASSIGNMENT

Review all the material you have written: narrative, description, process, and definition. How can this material be improved by illustration? Most likely the definition paper will be the one that can be most dramatically improved, because it is difficult to define an abstract concept without illustrating it. Research will be necessary as you search for accurately chosen illustrations to expand your paper. This means you will write at least one new literature review and a new source to your growing collection of Works Cited.

In addition to researching the perfect illustration, your own illustrations can also be added. They can be as brief as prepositional phrases (instead of just "angry" you might write, "angry as a rabid dog" to show the intensity of the anger) or as long as a parable of Jesus, all depending on what is needed to convey the intended meaning.

Finally, not all illustrations are narratives. Academic writing often uses **tables, figures,** and **examples**. All such illustrations should be inserted in the manuscript in the most logical and convenient place for the reader and documented as prescribed in the *MLA Handbook* (see pages 118-121). Make a list here of the ideas for illustration that immediately come to mind:

____

____

____

____

____

Write one page worth of illustration and insert it in the appropriate places in previously written materials. Highlight the added illustrative text and bring the full manuscript to class for a peer review. Since academic writing is usually produced on a black and white printer, avoid color highlights. Instead, follow the example here using the 25% gray highlight selected from the toolbar in Microsoft Word.

(name of person writing review) ____

PEER REVIEW: Have a fellow student read and evaluate the illustrations added to previously written material. The instructor is likely to assign partners for students who have done the same exercise.

Evaluate each illustration as follows:

____ Does the illustration illuminate the idea without introducing irrelevant material?

____ Is the illustration interesting?

____ Are an appropriate number of examples used?

____ Is the paper organized effectively with illustrations in the right places? If not, suggest where illustrations might be moved for better effect.

____ Identify the most boring part of this paper and delete it or make suggestions on how to make it more interesting.

____ Identify the most interesting part of this paper and tell the author why it is interesting.

____ Review for accuracy the MLA formatting of the Works Cited.

____ Review for accuracy the MLA formatting of the tables and figures, and examples (see *MLA Handbook* 118-121).

____ Cross out all first person singular (I, me, my, mine) and all second person (you, your) words to help the author achieve an appropriately objective paper.

Write a brief evaluation of the ways this paper is more effective now that it has been illustrated:

____

____

____

____

PLANNING THE REWRITE

Rewrite the illustration using the guidelines provided in the peer review. As you think about your illustrations, also contemplate the choice of words and the images used. A common mistake is to project the current meaning of a symbol backward onto past literature and therefore miss the intended meaning. For example, "gay" once meant "happy" in reference to attitude and "colorful" in reference to clothing. Make word choices that accurately communicate your intended meaning to the reader.

A second common mistake is to presume that the illustration accomplishes more than it actually does. Northrop Frye illustrates what is meant here in his observations regarding Samson in the Book of Judges:

> We may notice that Samson's name resembles early Semitic words for the sun, and that his story tells of a supernaturally powerful hero associated with the burning of crops, who eventually falls into a dark prison-house in the west. That the story shows structural or narrative analogies to the kind of story that might be suggested by the passage of the sun across the sky is true, and no storyteller worth his keep would try to eliminate such analogies. But to say that the Samson stories "derive from" a solar myth or that a solar myth "lies behind" them is to say more than anyone knows. (*Great Code* 35)

Review your illustrations to assure that you have made accurate word choices and realistic applications of images and ideas. Do not over state your case. In so doing you will gain credibility by avoiding the pitfall of saying more than anyone truly knows about the topic.

CHAPTER 6: CLASSIFICATION

Narrative tells a story, description stimulates the five senses, process shows how a thing is done, extended definitions explain aspects of a discipline, and all of them are more effective if well illustrated. **Classification** is yet another useful skill. To classify means to put with others of the same type, to "pigeon-hole," to create a category for organizing ideas. When advertisements are put into categories they are know as "classified ads," and when students are put in classes with others of similar age or ability, they have been classified. The entire network of information available on the web is accessible mainly through an elaborate system of classification.

A world without classification would be pure chaos. How would customers find anything in a grocery store if rugs were piled next to bananas? Classification places things in categories so life can be efficient and logical. Respond to the following questions to see the many ways in which grouping things into categories is fundamental to daily living.

List here the items generally placed in a closet: ____________________________________

____

List here the items generally placed in a kitchen: ___________________________________

____

List here the likely reactions if a stranger placed your kitchen items in your closet, or your closet items in your kitchen: ____

____

A man in need of a bicycle does not go shopping at an automotive dealership; a woman in need of cooking oil does not visit a furniture store. Make a list of ten important categories you use to make life at home, work, and church more efficient and logical.

1. ______________________________
2. ______________________________
3. ______________________________
4. ______________________________
5. ______________________________
6. ______________________________
7. ______________________________
8. ______________________________
9. ______________________________
10. ______________________________

The *MLA Handbook* models effective classification—it is easy to find the correct format for a Works Cited entry once the structure of the *MLA Handbook* is understood. Using the table of contents (v-xii) and the index (265-292), the college writing student is empowered to accurately document every conceivable source. Similarly, when writers place ideas in categories, they establish intelligent ways of thinking that make communicating the message to their audience efficient and logical.

CLASSIFICATION MODELS

Read the text below and try to identify the classification inherent in Isaiah 28:23-29:

> 23 Listen and hear my voice; pay attention and hear what I say. 24 When a
> farmer plows for planting, does he plow continually? Does he keep on breaking
> up and harrowing the soil? 25 When he has leveled the surface, does he not sow

caraway and scatter cummin? Does he not plant wheat in its place, barley in its plot, and spelt in its field? [26] His God instructs him and teaches him the right way.

[27] Caraway is not threshed with a sledge, nor is a cartwheel rolled over cummin; caraway is beaten out with a rod, and cummin with a stick. [28] Grain must be ground to make bread; so one does not go on threshing it forever. Though he drives the wheels of his threshing cart over it, his horses do not grind it.

[29] All this also comes from the LORD Almighty, wonderful in counsel and magnificent in wisdom.

ANALYSIS QUESTION:

1. Explain how the art of classification was useful to Isaiah, and why this passage makes more sense because of the classification employed.

The Apostle Paul was a master of classification as revealed in this passage:[1]

[5]Those who live according to the sinful nature have their minds set on what that nature desires; but those who live in accordance with the Spirit have their minds set on what the Spirit desires. [6]The mind of sinful man is death, but the mind controlled by the Spirit is life and peace; [7]the sinful mind is hostile to God. It does not submit to God's law, nor can it do so. [8]Those controlled by the sinful nature cannot please God.

[9]You, however, are controlled not by the sinful nature but by the Spirit, if the Spirit of God lives in you. And if anyone does not have the Spirit of Christ, he does not belong to Christ. [10]But if Christ is in you, your body is dead because of

[1] Notice two options for documenting biblical references. The first quote identifies the source (Isaiah 28:23-29) in the text, so no parenthetical reference is needed. The second quote from the Apostle Paul uses parenthetical reference at the end to identify the exact source.

> sin, yet your spirit is alive because of righteousness. [11]And if the Spirit of him
> who raised Jesus from the dead is living in you, he who raised Christ from the
> dead will also give life to your mortal bodies through his Spirit, who lives in you.
>
> [12]Therefore, brothers, we have an obligation—but it is not to the sinful
> nature, to live according to it. [13]For if you live according to the sinful nature, you
> will die; but if by the Spirit you put to death the misdeeds of the body, you will
> live, [14]because those who are led by the Spirit of God are sons of God. [15]For you
> did not receive a spirit that makes you a slave again to fear, but you received the
> Spirit of sonship. And by him we cry, "Abba, Father." [16]The Spirit himself
> testifies with our spirit that we are God's children. [17]Now if we are children, then
> we are heirs—heirs of God and co-heirs with Christ, if indeed we share in his
> sufferings in order that we may also share in his glory. (Romans 8:5-17)

ANALYSIS QUESTION

2. Make a list of the categories of classification used by Paul in the above passage.

Similarly, look for classification in a treatise on the supremacy of Christ:

> [15]He is the image of the invisible God, the firstborn over all creation. [16]For
> by him all things were created: things in heaven and on earth, visible and
> invisible, whether thrones or powers or rulers or authorities; all things were
> created by him and for him. [17]He is before all things, and in him all things hold
> together. [18]And he is the head of the body, the church; he is the beginning and the
> firstborn from among the dead, so that in everything he might have the
> supremacy. [19]For God was pleased to have all his fullness dwell in him, [20]and

> through him to reconcile to himself all things, whether things on earth or things in
> heaven, by making peace through his blood, shed on the cross.
>
> [21]Once you were alienated from God and were enemies in your minds
> because of your evil behavior. [22]But now he has reconciled you by Christ's
> physical body through death to present you holy in his sight, without blemish and
> free from accusation— [23]if you continue in your faith, established and firm, not
> moved from the hope held out in the gospel. This is the gospel that you heard and
> that has been proclaimed to every creature under heaven, and of which I, Paul,
> have become a servant. (Col.1:15-23 NIV)

ANALYSIS QUESTIONS

3. Explain how classification was a useful technique in this treatise on the supremacy of Christ.
4. Discuss how classification is typically done in your discipline. (Musicians may classify information differently than chemists; social scientists may do it differently than mathematicians; theologians may do it differently than artists.)
5. Explain how the classification already done by pioneers in your discipline has made it easier to understand and work within that discipline.

WRITING ASSIGNMENT

Follow guidelines given in class. Your instructor may not require a formal classification paper since this technique is generally used in conjunction with other structures. However, classification skills will be useful when you create a **comparison** paper, the subject of the next chapter.

CHAPTER 7: COMPARISON

Comparisons show relationships and can be done in either the alternating pattern or the block pattern. The alternating pattern quickly compares two things—sometimes within a single sentence: "The corn field is green whereas the wheat field is golden." A second example: "The tall stalks of corn shimmer as they rustle in the afternoon breeze while the swaying heads of wheat exude a deep luster as they bow under the blazing sun." The alternating pattern can also devote one sentence to the first thing and a another sentence to the second thing: "Pedro has three mules that carry water each morning and evening from the reservoir to the metal tank where grazing sheep conveniently drink within their pen without being threatened by wild dogs. However, his neighbor Pablo has rigged up a pump and hose running from the river to his barn where he gives the pigs their fill of water with the simple twist of a faucet handle." The following poem models how the alternating pattern carries with it an implicit comparison:

Our Love Is Not Donne Yet

Donne said 'tis not the bodies marry, but the minds
But I them both in you angelic find.
He said hope not for mind in women—at best
They just sweetness and wit possess.
But I with you found this plus all the rest.
Said he, lovers dream a rich and long delight
But get a winter-seeming summer's night,

While I with you (what have we done so right?)
Find sun and flowers all through winter's night.
He could not find the hidden mystery
But I have loved, and got, and told,
So as our love will blossom and unfold
I will with you abide as we grow old.
I found a love that's rich, and deep, and true,
A mighty gift from God reached me in you.[1]

In contrast to the above alternating pattern, the writer who describes corn for a full paragraph, then writes about wheat in the next paragraph, has adopted the block pattern of comparison. So has the publisher who devotes an entire chapter to Pedro's farming technique, followed by a chapter devoted to Pablo's farming technique. Mark Twain uses the block pattern in "Continued Perplexities," *Life on the Mississippi:*

> Now when I had mastered the language of this water and had come to know every trifling feature that bordered the great river as familiarly as I knew the letters of the alphabet, I had made a valuable acquisition. But I had lost something, too. I had lost something which could never be restored to me while I lived. All the grace, the beauty, the poetry, had gone out of the majestic river! I still kept in mind a certain wonderful sunset which I witnessed when steamboating was new to me. A broad expanse of the river was turned to blood; in the middle distance the red hue brightened into gold, through which a solitary log came floating, black and conspicuous; in one place a long, slanting mark lay

---

[1] Daniel V. Runyon, "Our Love Is Not Donne Yet," unpublished poem written for his wife on their wedding anniversary. The author compares his own experience with that described by John Donne in "Love's Alchemy."

sparkling upon the water; in another the surface was broken by boiling, tumbling rings that were as many-tinted as an opal; where the ruddy flush was faintest was a smooth spot that was covered with graceful circles and radiating lines, ever so delicately traced; the shore on our left was densely wooded, and the somber shadow that fell from this forest was broken in one place by a long, ruffled trail that shone like silver; and high above the forest wall a clean-stemmed dead tree waved a single leafy bough that glowed like a flame in the unobstructed splendor that was flowing from the sun. There were graceful curves, reflected images, woody heights, soft distances, and over the whole scene, far and near, the dissolving lights drifted steadily, enriching it every passing moment with new marvels of coloring.

I stood like one bewitched. I drank it in, in a speechless rapture. The world was new to me and I had never seen anything like this at home. But as I have said, a day came when I began to cease from noting the glories and the charms which the moon and the sun and the twilight wrought upon the river's face; another day came when I ceased altogether to note them. Then, if that sunset scene had been repeated, I should have looked upon it without rapture and should have commented upon it inwardly after this fashion: "This sun means that we are going to have wind tomorrow; that floating log means that the river is rising, small thanks to it; that slanting mark on the water refers to a bluff reef which is going to kill somebody's steamboat one of these nights, if it keeps on stretching out like that; those tumbling 'boils' show a dissolving bar and a changing channel there; the lines and circles in the slick water over yonder are a warning that that troublesome place is shoaling up dangerously; that silver streak in the shadow of the forest is the 'break' from a new snag and he has located himself in the very best place he could have found to fish for steamboats; that tall dead tree, with a single living branch, is not going to last long, and then how is a body ever going to get through this blind place at night without the friendly old landmark?"

No, the romance and beauty were all gone from the river. All the value any feature of it had for me now was the amount of usefulness it could furnish toward compassing the safe piloting of a steamboat. Since those days, I have pitied doctors from my heart. What does the lovely flush in a beauty's cheek mean to a doctor but a "break" that ripples above some deadly disease? Are not all her visible charms sown thick with what are to him the signs and symbols of hidden decay? Does he ever see her beauty at all, or doesn't he simply view her professionally and comment upon her unwholesome condition all to himself? And doesn't he sometimes wonder whether he has gained most or lost most by learning his trade? (64-66)

ANALYSIS QUESTIONS:

1. Write a paragraph speculating on why Twain chose the block pattern of comparison and the extremely long sentence in paragraph one.
2. Twain's seemingly endless sentences create a sense of flow so that the reader feels the steamboat under him and the length of the day and the dream-like qualities of the observations presented. If Twain had used the alternating pattern of comparison, what would be lost?

3. Explain what it would take to convert this portion of Twain's text from the block pattern to the alternating pattern of comparison. What could be gained by using the alternating pattern?

COMPARISON MODELS

The Apostle Paul used the art of comparison when he wrote to the Ephesians to help them understand their own transformed lives. Notice how he skillfully uses the past and present tense to create categories of comparison:

Ephesians 2 (New International Version)

[1]As for you, you were dead in your transgressions and sins, [2]in which you used to live when you followed the ways of this world and of the ruler of the kingdom of the air, the spirit who is now at work in those who are disobedient. [3]All of us also lived among them at one time, gratifying the cravings of our sinful nature and following its desires and thoughts. Like the rest, we were by nature objects of wrath. [4]But because of his great love for us, God, who is rich in mercy, [5]made us alive with Christ even when we were dead in transgressions—it is by grace you have been saved. [6]And God raised us up with Christ and seated us with him in the heavenly realms in Christ Jesus, [7]in order that in the coming ages he might show the incomparable riches of his grace, expressed in his kindness to us in Christ Jesus. [8]For it is by grace you have been saved, through faith—and this not from yourselves, it is the gift of God—[9]not by works, so that no one can boast. [10]For we are God's workmanship, created in Christ Jesus to do good works, which God prepared in advance for us to do.

[11]Therefore, remember that formerly you who are Gentiles by birth and called "uncircumcised" by those who call themselves "the circumcision" (that done in the body by the hands of men)—[12]remember that at that time you were separate from Christ, excluded from citizenship in Israel and foreigners to the covenants of the promise, without hope and without

God in the world. [13]But now in Christ Jesus you who once were far away have been brought near through the blood of Christ.

[14]For he himself is our peace, who has made the two one and has destroyed the barrier, the dividing wall of hostility, [15]by abolishing in his flesh the law with its commandments and regulations. His purpose was to create in himself one new man out of the two, thus making peace, [16]and in this one body to reconcile both of them to God through the cross, by which he put to death their hostility. [17]He came and preached peace to you who were far away and peace to those who were near. [18]For through him we both have access to the Father by one Spirit.

[19]Consequently, you are no longer foreigners and aliens, but fellow citizens with God's people and members of God's household, [20]built on the foundation of the apostles and prophets, with Christ Jesus himself as the chief cornerstone. [21]In him the whole building is joined together and rises to become a holy temple in the Lord. [22]And in him you too are being built together to become a dwelling in which God lives by his Spirit.

ANALYSIS QUESTION

4. In this comparison the author continually switches back and forth between the past tense ("you were") and the present tense ("but now"). Make two comprehensive lists organized in two columns. One list should show the situation as identified in the past tense features of Ephesians 2, the other of the present tense features.

Situation in the past	**Situation in the present**
______________________________	______________________________
______________________________	______________________________
______________________________	______________________________
______________________________	______________________________
______________________________	______________________________

Ephesians 5

[1]Be imitators of God, therefore, as dearly loved children [2]and live a life of love, just as Christ loved us and gave himself up for us as a fragrant offering and sacrifice to God.

[3]But among you there must not be even a hint of sexual immorality, or of any kind of impurity, or of greed, because these are improper for God's holy people. [4]Nor should there be obscenity, foolish talk or coarse joking, which are out of place, but rather thanksgiving. [5]For of this you can be sure: No immoral, impure or greedy person—such a man is an idolater—has any inheritance in the kingdom of Christ and of God. [6]Let no one deceive you with empty words, for because of such things God's wrath comes on those who are disobedient. [7]Therefore do not be partners with them.

[8]For you were once darkness, but now you are light in the Lord. Live as children of light [9](for the fruit of the light consists in all goodness, righteousness and truth) [10]and find out what pleases the Lord. [11]Have nothing to do with the fruitless deeds of darkness, but rather expose them. [12]For it is shameful even to mention what the disobedient do in secret. [13]But everything exposed by the light becomes visible, [14]for it is light that makes everything visible. This is why it is said:

"Wake up, O sleeper,
  rise from the dead,
and Christ will shine on you."

[15]Be very careful, then, how you live—not as unwise but as wise, [16]making the most of every opportunity, because the days are evil. [17]Therefore do not be foolish, but understand what the Lord's will is. [18]Do not get drunk on wine, which leads to debauchery. Instead, be filled with the Spirit. [19]Speak to one another with psalms, hymns and spiritual songs. Sing and make music in

your heart to the Lord, 20 always giving thanks to God the Father for everything, in the name of
our Lord Jesus Christ.

21 Submit to one another out of reverence for Christ.

22 Wives, submit to your husbands as to the Lord. 23 For the husband is the head of the wife as
Christ is the head of the church, his body, of which he is the Savior. 24 Now as the church submits
to Christ, so also wives should submit to their husbands in everything.

25 Husbands, love your wives, just as Christ loved the church and gave himself up for her 26 to
make her holy, cleansing her by the washing with water through the word, 27 and to present her to
himself as a radiant church, without stain or wrinkle or any other blemish, but holy and
blameless. 28 In this same way, husbands ought to love their wives as their own bodies. He who
loves his wife loves himself. 29 After all, no one ever hated his own body, but he feeds and cares
for it, just as Christ does the church—30 for we are members of his body. 31 "For this reason a man
will leave his father and mother and be united to his wife, and the two will become one flesh."
32 This is a profound mystery—but I am talking about Christ and the church. 33 However, each one
of you also must love his wife as he loves himself, and the wife must respect her husband.

ANALYSIS QUESTIONS

5. Write a paragraph explaining how the analogy to death and life make this comparison essay more convincing.
6. What other analogies besides death and life are used in the above texts, and how do they create a sense of comparison that helps the author communicate his message?
7. Write a paragraph explaining the ways in which you agree or disagree with this statement: "Opposites make attractive comparisons."

WRITING ASSIGNMENT

The role of novels in recent centuries has largely been replaced by movies in the current century. Many people today have watched more movies than they have read books. Writers must stay in touch with culture by watching these productions as well. Therefore, this assignment invites students to watch a movie and then write a paper in which they compare some aspect of that production with some aspect of their own field of study.

For example, a psychology major might compare the behavior of the main character in *Bruce Almighty* with the classic traits of a person suffering from Attention Deficit Disorder. A theology student could compare the way God is portrayed in the film with God as revealed in the New Testament, while a literature student would be more likely to compare the plot of the movie with a plot found in Shakespeare or Dickens. An art major might compare the use of lighting in the movie with the way light and shadows are used in a famous painting. Writing such a comparison will draw on all the skills learned in previous chapters while forcing writers to apply the knowledge and skills of their discipline to the world in which they live.

The first step is to select a movie to watch. The teacher is likely to make that decision and show the movie to the entire class. Here are some guidelines for watching it.

HOW TO WATCH A MOVIE

1. Do not expect to be entertained. Stay alert to every detail contained in the movie and come prepared to take notes as you watch.
2. Read the reviews and know what to expect so that you can gain the most from the viewing.
3. When reading reviews, be suspicious of the "objective" critic. When one film critic received a letter asking him to keep his opinions out of his reviews, he wrote back asking the writer to keep his opinions out of his letters. Opinions are what you are looking for in a review.

4. Do not expect the movie to be like the book. They are different media. Movies cannot do everything books can, although some try. Both the *Harry Potter* and *Lord of the Rings* movies make every effort to be as faithful to the books as possible. Modern special effects help make this possible.
5. Choose movies by actors and directors you already know you like.
6. Ignore the box office charts. Movies are not a sport, and the weekend's top film has won nothing except a lot of money. Not everyone willing to spend money on movies has your good taste—so do not trust the popularity test.
7. Be aware that *everything* in a movie is deliberate. Shots are filmed until the director is satisfied that his vision has been accurately recorded. Every movement of the frame and within the frame has a purpose. Ask yourself why each shot looks the way it does. Why is there a close-up here, a two-shot there? Common sense often dictates these things. A scene at a party might start with a shot of all the guests, then cut to a closer look at two guests deep in conversation, then cut to a close-up of a third person who notices that they are talking. The director needs to keep you oriented to what is going on as well as show you (tell you?) how to feel and think about every situation.
8. Be aware of symbols and their potential interpretations. A symbol is an image that creates a resonance in your mind. What does it symbolize? That depends on you and your mind. A dollar sign might symbolize wealth to you, greed to me, security to her, a mere price tag to him. The nice thing is that you can never be wrong about a symbol as long as you know what it means to you. You can only *speculate* on what it means to the director and actor, but you can *know* what it means to you.
9. Look for three kinds of action: internal, external, and symbolic. Internal action concerns the thoughts and feelings of characters. External action refers to all the actions taken by the

characters. Symbolic action refers to *how* things are done to represent a deeper meaning. If the boy kills the mouse and then laughs, it means something very different than if he kills the mouse because he must, and then weeps.

10. Notice the soundtrack. Be aware of how music is used to create mood and trigger emotions. Think about whether the sounds improve or detract from your viewing experience.
11. Realize that all good movies inspire conversations, rehashes, and arguments. Much of what you learn from a movie will come from discussions afterward with others who saw it.
12. Use both sides of your brain. The right side of your brain is devoted to sensory impressions, colors, music, and emotion. The left side of your brain deals with abstract thought, logic, philosophy, and analysis. A great movie will engage your right brain while you are watching it. It will engage your left brain after you have watched it.

THE ELEMENTS OF LITERATURE

Writing comparison papers based on a movie gives students experience integrating artistic and media events into scholarly research. The process of using material from a movie is not that different from using similar material from traditional literature or other print publications. Teachers of literature generally expect students to write about what they read. Below are typical things they look for:

1. Show how an author handled one element of a story.
2. Compare how two different works treat a particular element.
3. Weigh several elements and then determine the writer's intention.
4. Air your reactions to some work.

Most writing assignments feature one or more of the following elements: characterization, plot, point of view, setting, symbols, irony, and theme. Contemplate these concepts and answer the questions regarding these elements as you watch a movie. You are taking notes that will equip you to write an informed and effective paper.

Characterization: Authors deliberately develop their characters in a way that conveys a particular message or perspective. The better you understand the characters, the more accurately you will be able to analyze the literature as a whole. Most literature has a protagonist as well as a large assortment of other characters. Some of the questions to ask when studying characterization include the following:

1. How do the characters in a story behave?
2. What do they look like?
3. Where do their thoughts tend to linger?
4. What do they value in life?
5. How do they talk?
6. How do other people respond to them?
7. What are their personal habits?

Plot: Plot is the series of events that moves a narrative along. The stage is set, characters are introduced, and conflicts develop. Action gradually builds to a climax where events take a decisive turn and conflict is resolved in some way.

To organize plots, writers use several techniques. In foreshadowing, for example, the writer hints at later developments, thus creating interest and building suspense. When using flashback, the writer interrupts the flow of events to relate happenings that occurred before the point at which the story opened, then resumes the narrative at or near the point of interruption. Before writing about plot, answer these questions:

1. What are the key events of the story?

   Do they unfold in a conventional way or deviate from it in some way?

2. Identify where the writer uses foreshadowing or flashback.

   What purpose is achieved with these techniques?

3. Is the plot believable and effective, or weak in some way?

4. What are unique features of the plot?

5. Is this plot similar to another story with which you are familiar?

6. Select plot features to write about.

Point of View: This is the vantage point from which the writer views events. In first-person narration, someone in the work tells what happens. A third-person narrator stays completely out of the story. Most third-person narrators reveal the thoughts of just one character. Others, with limited omniscience, can enter the heads of several characters, while others display full omniscience and know everything. In contemporary fiction there is also another type of third-person narration—dramatic—in which a dramatic narrator moves about like a movie camera recording the actions and words of characters without revealing thoughts. Stories with surprise endings often use this technique. Explore these questions when writing about point of view:

1. What point of view is used? Why?

2. Is it suitable for the situation? Why or why not?

3. If the narration is first person, is the narrator reliable? What textual evidence supports the answer?

4. What focus would produce an effective paper? What textual evidence could support its discussion?

Setting: Setting locates characters in time, place, and culture so they can think, feel, and act against this background. Ask these questions about setting:

1. What are its key features?

2. What does the setting accomplish (create mood, reveal character, serve as a symbol, reinforce a point)? How does it accomplish these things?
3. In what ways does the setting seem realistic? If it does not seem realistic, why not?
4. What focus and textual evidence would produce an effective paper?

Symbols: Names, persons, objects, places, colors, or actions that have significance beyond their surface meaning are symbols. They can be very obvious (Mr. Grimm) or subtle, as an object representing a universal human emotion. A <u>private</u> symbol has special significance within a literary work but not outside it. For example, perhaps the feather that drifts through *Forest Gump* symbolizes the random way the main character's life and career have drifted forward. <u>Conventional</u> symbols are deeply rooted in culture, and almost everyone knows what they represent. The woman who wears a gold cross on a necklace symbolizes something very different from the man who has a swastika or devil's head tattoo on his shoulder. Answer these questions concerning symbols:

1. What symbols are used and where do they appear?
2. Are they *private* or *conventional*?
3. What do they appear to mean?
4. Do any of them undergo a change in meaning? If so, how and why?
5. Which symbol(s) could I discuss effectively?
6. What textual evidence would support my interpretation?

Irony: Ironic features are discrepancies between appearance and reality, expectation and outcome. Sometimes a character says one thing but means something else. When a college student tumbles out of bed, directly into yesterday's clothes, and out into the world without so much as a look in the mirror, a comment by a classmate that "you look great today" is probably thick with irony. Irony also results when the reader or a character recognizes something as important, but another character does not. Answer these questions regarding irony:

1. Where does irony occur?
2. What does it accomplish?
3. What could my thesis be, and how could I support it?

Theme: The theme is the controlling idea, observation, or insight about life conditions or terms of living (such as evil, pride, love). Many literary works suggest several themes—sometimes one primary motif and several related ones. Realize that the theme may not be stated at all. Rather, you figure it out based on the characters, action, setting and other components of the story. For example, a student might argue that the theme of Shakespeare's *Romeo and Juliet* is to emphasize the inherent dangers of dishonesty and disobedience. Ask these questions:

1. What are the themes of this work? Which of these should I write about? Are they stated or unstated?
2. If stated, what elements support them?
3. If unstated, what elements create them?
4. What, if any, thematic weaknesses are present?

Supplement your notes on the elements of literature with additional information gained by researching the authors, producers, and actors in the movie. Then it will be time to write the comparison paper. For guidelines on how to document a movie, look on page 273 under "films" in the index of the *MLA Handbook*.

RESEARCH USING BLOOM'S TAXONOMY

You will need additional sources of information to give credibility to your paper. The comparison paper is not intended merely for you to state your opinion, but to demonstrate that your opinion is valid. Therefore, to expand on an earlier example, the psychology student claiming that a character suffers from Attention Deficit Disorder will need to quote sources explaining the meaning and symptoms of this disorder. This is an opportunity for you to make further discoveries in your own field of growing expertise while also making application of that knowledge to the world around you.

The first level of writing literature reviews (covered in previous chapters) is to summarize, paraphrase, and quote from a source. This touches on the first two levels of learning as outlined in Bloom's Taxonomy. Bloom identified six levels of understanding from the simple recall or recognition of facts at the lowest level through increasingly more complex and abstract mental levels to the highest order classified as evaluation (Dalton).

Assignment: Select a source containing valuable information to include in your comparison paper. Study that source in depth, read footnotes or endnotes, and look up in a reliable dictionary any words you do not understand. Then write a literature review that includes the following:

1 & 2: Knowledge and Comprehension: Briefly summarize the source. If it is fiction, explain to your audience who the characters are and what they represent (choose a particular audience you wish to speak to).

3, 4 & 5: ***Application, Analysis, and Synthesis:*** Explain the context and audience of the original source. What did the material *mean* to the author and to his immediate audience? What is it likely to mean to readers today? What does it mean to you?

6. Evaluation: Appraise the quality and success of the material, perhaps comparing it with other similar materials that are more (or less) effective in achieving the same goals. How is this material useful in strengthening your comparison paper?

(name of person writing review) ____

PEER REVIEW: Have a fellow student read and evaluate the comparison paper. It will be ideal if that student has also written a comparison paper about the same movie.

Classification (from chapter 6)

1. Has the author classified the aspect of the movie in question (placed it in a category)?

____yes ____no If not, suggest a category: ______________________________

2. Has the author classified the thing the movie is being compared with? ____yes ____no

    A. Are they in the same class or category? If so, this paper should compare similarities.

    B. Are they in different classes or categories? If so, this paper should contrast differences.

Comparison: Showing Relationships

3. Is the comparison using the block pattern or the alternating pattern?

    ____ block ____ alternating ____ a combination of the two

4. Does the author use an analogy or illustration (from chapter 5)? ____ yes ____no

If not, is one needed to help the reader understand this comparison?

5. Does the paper consider all points of similarity and difference that relate to its purpose?

6. Are the comparisons arranged effectively?

Writing About Literature

7. Identify the elements of literature being compared in this paper and write them in the margins of the paper at appropriate places. Circle all that apply.

    character plot point of view setting symbols irony theme

8. Identify the types of action being compared in this paper and write them in the margins of the paper at appropriate places. Circle all that apply.

    external action internal action symbolic action

9. Evaluate how successfully the writer has applied Bloom's Taxonomy to the additional sources used: evaluation, synthesis, analysis, application, understanding, knowledge. Identify points where you feel additional application of Bloom's Taxonomy would strengthen the paper.

General Evaluation

10. Read just the introduction and the conclusion. Edit so the two paragraphs hang together.

11. Help with transitions so each paragraph clearly and smoothly relates to those that precede and follow it.

12. Fix sentences that are not clearly expressed or logically constructed.

13. Omit needless words.

14. What can be done to make this comparison smell, taste, feel, look, and sound better?

____

____

15. A minimum of four sources are required. (The movie itself is one of them.) How appropriate are the three additional sources to the point of this paper? Suggest changes if appropriate.

____

____

16. Review the MLA format, punctuation and grammar, and content of parenthetical references and Works Cited for accuracy.

PLANNING THE REWRITE

Rewrite this paper and turn it in to the professor when due. At about this point students frequently ask, "How do I cite indirect sources—information found in one source but originating in another source?" In most scholarly work writers are required to go back to the original source and cite only that reference. Once they pull the original source and have looked up the reference and read it for themselves, they have verified the accuracy and can avoid mentioning the path leading them to that source. However, some professors permit undergraduate students to cite the original source and then add, "qtd. in...." An example is provided in the footnote below.[2] See the *MLA Handbook* page 226 for additional guidance.

A second difficulty with this rewrite may have to do with questions on how to document quotes within movies or quotes by reviewers. See *MLA Handbook* B. 1.6 for how to format a review footnote, and see "films" in the index (page 273) for guidance in locating documentation guidelines for a movie.

AVOIDING PLAGIARISM EXERCISE

Write the following quote in your own words: "There is enough light for those who want to see and enough darkness for those of a contrary disposition." —Pascal

____

____

____

____

____

[2] Hypothetical example of one source quoting a second source: C. S. Lewis, *The Four Loves* (Oxford: Clarendon, 1967) 59, qtd. in Howard Snyder and Daniel Runyon, *Decoding The Church: Mapping the DNA of Christ's Body* (Grand Rapids: Baker, 2002) 218.

CHAPTER 8: MEDIA ANALYSIS

The ability to analyze the media became a vital skill with the development of the "mass media" in the past few centuries. No such thing existed prior to the 1440s when Johann Gutenberg introduced movable type in Germany. The influence of Gutenberg's printing abilities was recognized immediately, and authorities quickly erected barriers to control its influence on public opinion. Printers and writers in the English-speaking world struggled until 1700 to win the mere right to print. They fought for another century to protect that liberty and to win the right to criticize in print. The right to report news came equally slowly.

The freedom to print, to criticize, and to report in a way that defends the people's right to know is continually challenged today. In the United States, freedom of the press is intertwined with other basic freedoms—freedom of speech, freedom of assembly, and freedom of petition. Upon these freedoms rests the freedom of religious expression, freedom of political thought and action, and freedom of intellectual growth and communication of information and ideas.

The founding fathers of the United States worked to create a society with a government of the people, by the people, and for the people. The media is the chief instrument though which any such society can talk to itself, and therefore the people will fail to govern themselves successfully when they lose the ability to intelligently evaluate the accuracy, fairness, and truthfulness of the media.

The media has evolved from the printing press through radio, television, and the internet, but the premise remains the same, as explained by Thomas Jefferson, third President of the

United States, in a letter to Richard Price: "Whenever the people are well informed, they can be trusted with their own government." Jefferson's confidence in the value of the free marketplace of thought is revealed in this letter:

> I am persuaded that the good sense of the people will always be found to be the best army. They may be led astray for a moment, but will soon correct themselves. The people are the only censors of their governors; and even their errors will tend to keep these to the true principles of their institution. To punish these errors too severely would be to suppress the only safeguard of the public liberty. The way to prevent these irregular interpositions of the people, is to give them full information of their affairs through the channel of the public papers, and to contrive that those papers should penetrate to the whole mass of the people. The basis of our government being the opinion of the people, the very first object should be to keep that right; and were it left to me to decide whether we should have a government without newspapers, or newspapers without a government, I should not hesitate a moment to prefer the latter.[1]

The internet has created a global communications network making it vital for people in any country with access to that information to learn the skills of media analysis. All the writing and thinking skills taught in this text must be brought into play here. The media analysis assignment will draw on **narrative** writing, **description** skills, and the ability to **define** and **illustrate** a concept. The ability to **classify** information and understand **process** also plays an important role in successful media analysis.

---

[1] Jefferson wrote many variations on this theme over a 19-year span from 1792-1811. The occasions included letters to George Hammond, May 29, 1792; William Duane, Mar. 28, 1811; and to Congress, Dec. 2, 1806. This hand-written letter is available for viewing online at <http://memory.loc.gov/ammem/collections/jefferson_papers>.

A media event is anything that happens and is reported in any media format. One such event occurred on Saturday, March 4, 1865, in Washington, D.C., when President Abraham Lincoln delivered his Second Inaugural Address. Weeks of wet weather had turned Pennsylvania Avenue into a sea of mud and standing water where thousands of citizens stood to hear him speak. It was a troubled time dominated by years of civil war. In little more than a month, the President would be assassinated.

Media Sample: Abraham Lincoln's Second Inaugural Address

Fellow-Countrymen:

At this second appearing to take the oath of the Presidential office there is less occasion for an extended address than there was at the first. Then a statement somewhat in detail of a course to be pursued seemed fitting and proper. Now, at the expiration of four years, during which public declarations have been constantly called forth on every point and phase of the great contest which still absorbs the attention and engrosses the energies of the nation, little that is new could be presented. The progress of our arms, upon which all else chiefly depends, is as well known to the public as to myself, and it is, I trust, reasonably satisfactory and encouraging to all. With high hope for the future, no prediction in regard to it is ventured.

On the occasion corresponding to this four years ago all thoughts were anxiously directed to an impending civil war. All dreaded it, all sought to avert it. While the inaugural address was being delivered from this place, devoted altogether to saving the Union without war, urgent agents were in the city seeking to destroy it without war—seeking to dissolve the Union and divide effects by negotiation. Both parties deprecated war, but one of them would make war rather than let the nation survive, and the other would accept war rather than let it perish, and the war came.

One-eighth of the whole population were colored slaves, not distributed generally over the Union, but localized in the southern part of it. These slaves constituted a peculiar and powerful interest. All knew that this interest was somehow the cause of the war. To strengthen, perpetuate, and extend this interest was the object for which the insurgents would rend the Union even by war, while the Government claimed no right to do more than to restrict the territorial enlargement of it.

Neither party expected for the war the magnitude or the duration which it has already attained. Neither anticipated that the cause of the conflict might cease with or even before the conflict itself should cease. Each looked for an easier triumph, and a result less fundamental and astounding. Both read the same Bible and pray to the same God, and each invokes His aid against the other. It may seem strange that any men should dare to ask a just God's assistance in wringing their bread from the sweat of other men's faces, but let us judge not, that we be not judged.

The prayers of both could not be answered. That of neither has been answered fully. The Almighty has His own purposes. "Woe unto the world because of offenses; for it must needs be that offenses come, but woe to that man by whom the offense cometh." If we shall suppose that American slavery is one of those offenses which, in the providence of God, must needs come, but which, having continued through His appointed time, He now wills to remove, and that He gives to both North and South this terrible war as the woe due to those by whom the offense came, shall we discern therein any departure from those divine attributes which the believers in a living God always ascribe to Him?

Fondly do we hope, fervently do we pray, that this mighty scourge of war may speedily pass away. Yet, if God wills that it continue until all the wealth piled by the bondsman's two hundred and fifty years of unrequited toil shall be sunk, and until every drop of blood drawn with the lash shall be paid by another drawn with the sword, as was said three thousand years ago, so still it must be said "the judgments of the Lord are true and righteous altogether."

With malice toward none, with charity for all, with firmness in the right as God gives us to see the right, let us strive on to finish the work we are in, to bind up the nation's wounds, to care for him who shall have borne the battle and for his widow and his orphan, to do all which may achieve and cherish a just and lasting peace among ourselves and with all nations.

ANALYSIS QUESTIONS

1. Write a paragraph exploring how TV commentators would likely respond today if they were covering this very short inaugural address.
2. Write your reaction to the fact that President Lincoln quotes the Bible, talks about the sovereignty of God, and explores the complexities of unanswered prayer as integral parts of this auspicious speech.
3. The theme of "just war" underlies Lincoln's thoughts. How should this concept play into any interpretation of this media event?

MEDIA ANALYSIS MODELS

If "media" can be broadly defined as "news" of any public event, then it occurred daily in the ancient world, and public opinion flourished although it had no technology to quickly spread such opinions around the globe. The arrest and murder of Jesus is perhaps the most notorious media event ever recorded by eyewitnesses. Excerpts of Matthew's account appear below along with analysis questions to help modern readers apply media analysis skills to the event.

Matthew 26:1-16 (The Message)

When Jesus finished saying these things, he told his disciples, "You know that Passover comes in two days. That's when the Son of Man will be betrayed and handed over for crucifixion."

At that very moment, the party of high priests and religious leaders was meeting in the chambers of the Chief Priest named Caiaphas, conspiring to seize Jesus by stealth and kill him. They agreed that it should not be done during Passover Week. "We don't want a riot on our hands," they said.

When Jesus was at Bethany, a guest of Simon the Leper, a woman came up to him as he was eating dinner and anointed him with a bottle of very expensive perfume. When the disciples saw what was happening, they were furious. "That's criminal! This could have been sold for a lot and the money handed out to the poor."

When Jesus realized what was going on, he intervened. "Why are you giving this woman a hard time? She has just done something wonderfully significant for me. You will have the poor with you every day for the rest of your lives, but not me. When she poured this perfume on my body, what she really did was anoint me for burial. You can be sure that wherever in the whole world the Message is preached, what she has just done is going to be remembered and admired."

That is when one of the Twelve, the one named Judas Iscariot, went to the cabal of high priests and said, "What will you give me if I hand him over to you?" They settled on thirty silver pieces. He began looking for just the right moment to hand him over.

ANALYSIS QUESTIONS

4. Identify which characters described above genuinely understood what was going on, and summarize what each one apparently understood about the event.
5. Identify which characters have the greatest influence on how the event is portrayed by the "media." Summarize what you think their "spin" will be.

Matthew 26:57-68

The gang that had seized Jesus led him before Caiaphas the Chief Priest, where the religion scholars and leaders had assembled. Peter followed at a safe distance until they got to the Chief

Priest's courtyard. Then he slipped in and mingled with the servants, watching to see how things would turn out.

The high priests, conspiring with the Jewish Council, tried to cook up charges against Jesus in order to sentence him to death. But even though many stepped up, making up one false accusation after another, nothing was believable.

Finally two men came forward with this: "He said, 'I can tear down this Temple of God and after three days rebuild it.'"

The Chief Priest stood up and said, "What do you have to say to the accusation?"

Jesus kept silent.

Then the Chief Priest said, "I command you by the authority of the living God to say if you are the Messiah, the Son of God."

Jesus was curt: "You yourself said it. And that's not all. Soon you'll see it for yourself:

> The Son of Man seated at the right hand of the Mighty One,
>
> Arriving on the clouds of heaven."

At that, the Chief Priest lost his temper, ripping his robes, yelling, "He blasphemed! Why do we need witnesses to accuse him? You all heard him blaspheme! Are you going to stand for such blasphemy?"

They all said, "Death! That seals his death sentence."

Then they were spitting in his face and banging him around. They jeered as they slapped him: "Prophesy, Messiah: Who hit you that time?"

ANALYSIS QUESTION

6. This report comes from Matthew, a disciple of Jesus. How might an official report from the Chief Priest read differently? What details might be added or eliminated, and why would they be likely to make these changes?

Matthew 27:11-26

Jesus was placed before the governor, who questioned him: "Are you the 'King of the Jews'?"

Jesus said, "If you say so."

But when the accusations rained down hot and heavy from the high priests and religious leaders, he said nothing. Pilate asked him, "Do you hear that long list of accusations? Aren't you going to say something?" Jesus kept silence—not a word from his mouth. The governor was impressed, really impressed.

It was an old custom during the Feast for the governor to pardon a single prisoner named by the crowd. At the time, they had the infamous Jesus Barabbas in prison. With the crowd before him, Pilate said, "Which prisoner do you want me to pardon: Jesus Barabbas, or Jesus the so-called Christ?" He knew it was through sheer spite that they had turned Jesus over to him.

While court was still in session, Pilate's wife sent him a message: "Don't get mixed up in judging this noble man. I've just been through a long and troubled night because of a dream about him."

Meanwhile, the high priests and religious leaders had talked the crowd into asking for the pardon of Barabbas and the execution of Jesus.

The governor asked, "Which of the two do you want me to pardon?"

They said, "Barabbas!"

"Then what do I do with Jesus, the so-called Christ?"

They all shouted, "Nail him to a cross!"

He objected, "But for what crime?"

But they yelled all the louder, "Nail him to a cross!"

When Pilate saw that he was getting nowhere and that a riot was imminent, he took a basin of water and washed his hands in full sight of the crowd, saying, "I'm washing my hands of responsibility for this man's death. From now on, it's in your hands. You're judge and jury."

The crowd answered, "We'll take the blame, we and our children after us."

Then he pardoned Barabbas. But he had Jesus whipped, and then handed over for crucifixion.

ANALYSIS QUESTION

7. How is the system of justice presided over by Pilate similar to the way prisoners are treated where you live? How is it different?

Matthew 27:35-44

After they had finished nailing him to the cross and were waiting for him to die, they whiled away the time by throwing dice for his clothes. Above his head they had posted the criminal charge against him: THIS IS JESUS, THE KING OF THE JEWS. Along with him, they also crucified two criminals, one to his right, the other to his left. People passing along the road jeered, shaking their heads in mock lament: "You bragged that you could tear down the Temple and then rebuild it in three days—so show us your stuff! Save yourself! If you're really God's Son, come down from that cross!"

The high priests, along with the religion scholars and leaders, were right there mixing it up with the rest of them, having a great time poking fun at him: "He saved others—he can't save himself! King of Israel, is he? Then let him get down from that cross. We'll all become believers then! He was so sure of God—well, let him rescue his 'Son' now—if he wants him! He did claim to be God's Son, didn't he?"

… From noon to three, the whole earth was dark. Around mid-afternoon Jesus groaned out of the depths, crying loudly, "Eli, Eli, lama sabachthani?" which means "My God, my God, why have you abandoned me?"

Some bystanders who heard him said, "He's calling for Elijah." One of them ran and got a sponge soaked in sour wine and lifted it on a stick so he could drink. The others joked, "Don't be in such a hurry. Let's see if Elijah comes and saves him."

But Jesus, again crying out loudly, breathed his last.

At that moment, the Temple curtain was ripped in two, top to bottom. There was an earthquake, and rocks were split in pieces. What's more, tombs were opened up, and many bodies of believers asleep in their graves were raised. (After Jesus' resurrection, they left the tombs, entered the holy city, and appeared to many.)

The captain of the guard and those with him, when they saw the earthquake and everything else that was happening, were scared to death. They said, "This has to be the Son of God!"

There were also quite a few women watching from a distance, women who had followed Jesus from Galilee in order to serve him. Among them were Mary Magdalene, Mary the mother of James and Joseph, and the mother of the Zebedee brothers.

ANALYSIS QUESTIONS

8. Some countries do not permit more than one point of view when reporting such an event. What sort of trouble might Matthew be in if he publishes this portrayal of the behavior of the religious authorities?
9. If not published for the general public, how might this information be circulated?

Matthew 27:62-66

After sundown, the high priests and Pharisees arranged a meeting with Pilate. They said, "Sir, we just remembered that that liar announced while he was still alive, 'After three days I will be raised.' We've got to get that tomb sealed until the third day. There's a good chance his disciples will come and steal the corpse and then go around saying, 'He's risen from the dead.' Then we'll be worse off than before, the final deceit surpassing the first."

Pilate told them, “You will have a guard. Go ahead and secure it the best you can.” So they went out and secured the tomb, sealing the stone and posting guards.

ANALYSIS QUESTION

10. This passage models the common practice of authorities who tend to want to put a "spin" or bias on public opinion to justify their own actions. Evaluate the actions of both the Pharisees and Pilate in this regard.

    A. Actions taken by the Pharisees:

    B. Actions taken by Pilate:

Matthew 28:1-10

After the Sabbath, as the first light of the new week dawned, Mary Magdalene and the other Mary came to keep vigil at the tomb. Suddenly the earth reeled and rocked under their feet as God’s angel came down from heaven, came right up to where they were standing. He rolled back the stone and then sat on it. Shafts of lightning blazed from him. His garments shimmered snow-white. The guards at the tomb were scared to death. They were so frightened, they couldn’t move.

The angel spoke to the women: “There is nothing to fear here. I know you’re looking for Jesus, the One they nailed to the cross. He is not here. He was raised, just as he said. Come and look at the place where he was placed.

“Now, get on your way quickly and tell his disciples, ‘He is risen from the dead. He is going on ahead of you to Galilee. You will see him there.’ That’s the message.”

The women, deep in wonder and full of joy, lost no time in leaving the tomb. They ran to tell the disciples. Then Jesus met them, stopping them in their tracks. “Good morning!” he said. They fell to their knees, embraced his feet, and worshiped him. Jesus said, “You’re holding on to me for dear life! Don't be frightened like that. Go tell my brothers that they are to go to Galilee, and that I'll meet them there."

ANALYSIS QUESTION

11. Matthew may not have been at all the events described above, but as one of the disciples "they ran to tell," he would have been among the first to hear the report. Compare his situation with that of a modern reporter who must interview eyewitnesses to get a report.

Matthew 28:11-15

Meanwhile, the guards had scattered, but a few of them went into the city and told the high priests everything that had happened. They called a meeting of the religious leaders and came up with a plan: They took a large sum of money and gave it to the soldiers, bribing them to say, "His disciples came in the night and stole the body while we were sleeping." They assured them, "If the governor hears about your sleeping on duty, we will make sure you don't get blamed." The soldiers took the bribe and did as they were told. That story, cooked up in the Jewish High Council, is still going around.

ANALYSIS QUESTIONS

12. Is understanding and interpreting an event that occurred more than a century ago easier than evaluating a current event in the same way? Answer "yes" or "no" and explain why.
13. Imagine the difficulties modern media analysts would encounter if they faced trying to understand the crucifixion. What would they be most likely to misunderstand about this event? Why?
14. Tell a true story from your own experience where you know the truth was different from that which was generally accepted as true.

15. How did Matthew's skill as a discerning media analyst help assure the accuracy of the Bible?

16. How will you imitate the work of Matthew in order to write your own perceptive and reliable media analysis paper?

WRITING ASSIGNMENT

It doesn't matter whether the media critics are standing in the mud listening to Abraham Lincoln's Second Inaugural Address in person, witnessing the resurrection of Jesus from the dead, or reading an editorial on an internet blog. Whether the media event is a speech, a TV show, a news clip, or an article in a newspaper or magazine, the questions wise media analysts ask and the notes they take are similar and should include those suggested in the form below.

In order to fill out this form, it is first necessary to identify the media event you wish to evaluate. Select a recent happening in your field of interest. You will most likely find this information in a scholarly journal devoted to your field of study or a specialized internet news service focused on your discipline. Do not use a movie for your media event since that was the subject of the assignment for the last chapter. However, any other media event is a fair target, whether in print or visual media. Once you have located a media event of great personal interest, write the information requested below in a journal or computer file.

Name of production or name of article ______________________________

Authors ______________________________

Names of important people ______________________________

Names of important places ______________________________

Names of important events (with dates and locations) ______________________________

Key ideas and themes presented ______________________________

Summary of production ______________________________

Good media analysis questions to consider include the following:

1. How is the production structured?
2. What is the author/producer trying to say? Paraphrase a key element of the content.
3. What is the author's bias or worldview? That is to say, what are you being told to believe, or what "spin" is placed on the facts presented?
4. What are your personal feelings and reaction to the work?
5. Now that you have collected useful notes, you are ready for the prewriting exercise.

PRE-WRITING EXERCISE

1. Accurately document the media event/article you will critique based on guidelines in the *MLA Handbook* by writing a Works Cited entry in correct format.
2. Do you understand the *assumptions* (worldview) that shape the production being analyzed? Are the assumptions stated or unstated? What are they?
3. What is the fundamental argument of the media event being analyzed?
4. Is the argument *valid*: does the conclusion *necessarily* follow? (See Chapter 10 for a discussion of what constitutes a valid argument.) Outline the argument.
5. If the argument is valid, are the premises to the argument *true*? Identify the premises.
6. Can you identify any *logical fallacies* in the media production being analyzed? (See Chapter 10 for a list of logical fallacies and their definitions.) List them.
7. How will you take advantage of the logical fallacies to make your own argument stronger? Be sure you do not fall into logical fallacies of your own.

Give Your Analysis Credibility

Now you are ready to write your analysis of the media event. By the time you finish the first draft, it should become clear that you are not a recognized authority on the topic you have chosen to address. Therefore, you do not have the credibility to make the claims you may wish to make. The way to gain credibility is to align yourself with authorities in your field of study who are respected experts. Skilled writers know how to back up a point they want to make by identifying it with what the experts have already said. This is the beauty and value of research. To say "I think that …" has practically no value compared with being able to write, "Einstein's theory of relativity provides convincing evidence that…."

To carry out your research, follow the "Research Using Bloom's Taxonomy" guidelines provided in Chapter 7. Assume that your professor will require three literature reviews along with the final paper (show your work!). Be sure to use accurate parenthetical references with every source you use, and include each source in the Works Cited, just as you learned to do on all previous assignments. Make sure to carefully follow all formatting and punctuation guidelines provided in the *MLA Handbook.*

(name of person writing review) ____

PEER REVIEW: Have a fellow student read and evaluate the media analysis.

1. Read entire paper:

a. As you read, bracket each section of **objective** information and write "objective" or "facts" in the margin. (Review Chapter One for a summary of objective, subjective, and interpretive information.)

b. Bracket each section of **subjective** information and write "subjective" or "opinion" in the margin.

c. Bracket each section of **interpretive** information and write "interpretation" or "author's conclusion" in the margin.

____ Check to make sure each piece of **objective** information is adequately documented (with correctly written parenthetical reference and bibliography).

____ Check to make sure each piece of **subjective** information is sufficiently plausible, convincing, and adequately backed up with objective information.

____ Check to make sure each piece of **interpretive** information has been arrived at *in a logical manner* and is adequately backed up with subjective and objective information.

Does the writer show evidence of truly understanding the *assumptions* (worldview) that shaped the production being analyzed? Are the assumptions stated or unstated? What are they?

____

____

____

____

If the writer is building some argument concerning the media event being analyzed, is the argument inductive or deductive?

Inductive argument follows some form of the scientific method that explores the extent to which a thing is *probably* true based on the evidence (see Chapter 11 for more details).

Deductive argument follows a syllogism: If one thing is true, and if a second thing is true, then this conclusion is sound (see Chapter 10 for more details). If the argument is deductive, is the argument *valid* (does the conclusion n*ecessarily* follow)? Are the premises to the argument *true*?

Can you identify any *logical fallacies* in the writer's analysis of the media production? (See Chapter 10 for a list of logical fallacies). If so, list them here:

Make suggestions to the author on how to improve this paper in the space below.

PLANNING THE REWRITE

Your media analysis paper is based on published sources, and the ultimate goal of writing such a paper is to see it published. Therefore, it will be helpful at this time to compare your own writing with that of the published materials on which you based your work.

1. How does your writing style compare with the published articles? Is it better or worse? In what ways?
2. How does the content of your paper compare with the published articles?
3. How does your argument compare with the published articles? Is it more convincing, or less so? How can you tell?

INVISIBLE MAN

As you write your final draft, remember to employ the various writing skills encouraged in earlier chapters to make your paper powerful. When Ralph Ellison wrote *Invisible Man,* he used such skills to describe one aspect of a media event, a solo at a vespers service at a southern college. Notice his powers of description and his ability to capture the climate:

> As the organ voices died, I saw a thin brown girl arise noiselessly with the rigid control of a modern dancer, high in the upper rows of the choir, and begin to sing a cappella. She began softly, as though singing to herself of emotions of utmost privacy, a sound not addressed to the gathering, but which they overheard almost against her will….
>
> I saw the guests on the platform turn to look behind them, to see the thin brown girl in white choir robe standing high against the organ pipes, herself become before our eyes a pipe of contained, controlled and sublimated anguish, a thin plain face transformed by music. I could not understand the words, but only the mood, sorrowful, vague and ethereal, of the singing. It throbbed with

> nostalgia, regret and repentance, and I sat with a lump in my throat as she sank down; not a sitting but a controlled collapsing, as though she were balancing, sustaining the simmering bubble of her final tone by some delicate rhythm of her heart's blood, or by some mystic concentration of her being, focused upon the sound through the contained liquid of her large uplifted eyes. There was no applause, only the appreciation of a profound silence. (116-117)

With such writing Ellison has simultaneously analyzed the event and also pushed himself to a higher level of expression, capturing mood and feeling and spirit as well as facts. Use the insights above and the suggestions provided by the peer review for guidance as you rewrite your media analysis paper and turn it in for a grade.

CHAPTER 9: CAUSE AND EFFECT ARGUMENT

Understanding cause and effect is basic to logic, and knowing how to think logically is the foundation for argument. This chapter explores the cause and effect system of reasoning. Chapter 10 moves beyond cause and effect to the "deductive argument" system of reasoning based on linear logic rooted in ancient Greek thought. Chapter 11 will explore the "inductive argument" thought process common in much of the world where Duane Elmer's observation rings true, that "people from various cultures reason differently" (150).

Cause and effect reasoning can result in persuasive writing. When it is established that one thing always results in another thing, it becomes possible to explain why things are as they are. Much scientific research is based on cause and effect reasoning, and it is possible that students who wrote a process paper based on the scientific method summarized in Chapter 3 were working primarily with a cause and effect situation.

Writing a paper on cause and effect becomes somewhat complicated because things are seldom as simple as they appear. Consider this statement: "If a person heats water, then it will boil when it reaches 212 degrees Fahrenheit." This is a simple cause and effect statement. But it is only true at sea level, and water actually boils at increasingly lower temperatures at higher altitudes. People living at 5500 feet altitude in Colorado will find water boils there at about 202 degrees. This does not mean the cause and effect statement is wrong, just that it is conditional. Much of the work of writing in cause and effect format has to do with explaining all the conditions that make the original statement true.

Also keep in mind that multiple causes often contribute to a single effect. Why is Ming-Yau six feet tall although his parents are only five feet tall? The cause is not only because he inherited the physique of his grandfather who was much taller than his mother, but also because he was given daily vitamins and nutritional food of excellent quality and variety throughout his formative years, whereas both of his parents had only a daily portion of rice to eat their first 15 years of life. To identify only one cause for the effect oversimplifies the situation.

Another frequent mistake is to assume that because one event occurs before another, the second effect was caused by the first action. A new leader is elected and then a drought causes economic hardship, but the election results most likely did not cause the drought, which would have come no matter which candidate was chosen.[1] Superstitions are often the result of this fallacy of apparent but not actual cause and effect.

A final reasoning error occurs when causes are confused with their effects. A young child might observe a tree limb swaying and believe it is making the wind blow. Adults with more knowledge of the world explain that actually it is the wind that causes the tree to sway. Yet on an even larger scale, the child may be right. Huge rain forests in Brazil create weather patterns by putting large volumes of moisture in the air which may in fact cause the wind to blow.

Cause and effect drives the plot of many stories. Hermann, the protagonist in the famous Russian author Alexander Pushkin's short story *The Queen of Spades,* says in two places regarding his reluctance to gamble, "I am not in the position to sacrifice the necessary in the hope of winning the superfluous" (1, 10). When he violates this principle with an audacious gambling risk, his life is shattered. Pushkin comprehended the power of cause and effect reasoning and used it as the core of a powerful plot. It is equally useful as the core of a powerful college writing essay.

---

[1] This is an example of the "Post hoc, ergo propter hoc" fallacy described in Chapter 10.

CAUSE AND EFFECT MODELS

1. **Analysis question:** Based on the readings below, make a chart that lists causes in the left hand column and their effects in the right hand column. Be careful to avoid the fallacies discussed above of multiple causes, confusing chronology with cause and effect, and mistaking effects for causes.

James 4:7-10 (New Revised Standard Version)

7 Submit yourselves therefore to God. Resist the devil, and he will flee from you. 8 Draw near to God, and he will draw near to you. Cleanse your hands, you sinners, and purify your hearts, you double-minded. 9 Lament and mourn and weep. Let your laughter be turned into mourning and your joy into dejection. 10 Humble yourselves before the Lord, and he will exalt you.

James 4:7-10 Chart

Causes	**Effects**
____________________	____________________

John 3 (New International Version)

1 Now there was a man of the Pharisees named Nicodemus, a member of the Jewish ruling council. 2 He came to Jesus at night and said, "Rabbi, we know you are a teacher who has come from God. For no one could perform the miraculous signs you are doing if God were not with him."

3 In reply Jesus declared, "I tell you the truth, no one can see the kingdom of God unless he is born again."

____

[4]"How can a man be born when he is old?" Nicodemus asked. "Surely he cannot enter a second time into his mother's womb to be born!"

[5]Jesus answered, "I tell you the truth, no one can enter the kingdom of God unless he is born of water and the Spirit. [6]Flesh gives birth to flesh, but the Spirit gives birth to spirit. [7]You should not be surprised at my saying, 'You must be born again.' [8]The wind blows wherever it pleases. You hear its sound, but you cannot tell where it comes from or where it is going. So it is with everyone born of the Spirit."

[9]"How can this be?" Nicodemus asked.

[10]"You are Israel's teacher," said Jesus, "and do you not understand these things? [11]I tell you the truth, we speak of what we know, and we testify to what we have seen, but still you people do not accept our testimony. [12]I have spoken to you of earthly things and you do not believe; how then will you believe if I speak of heavenly things? [13]No one has ever gone into heaven except the one who came from heaven—the Son of Man. [14]Just as Moses lifted up the snake in the desert, so the Son of Man must be lifted up, [15]that everyone who believes in him may have eternal life.

[16]"For God so loved the world that he gave his one and only Son, that whoever believes in him shall not perish but have eternal life. [17]For God did not send his Son into the world to condemn the world, but to save the world through him. [18]Whoever believes in him is not condemned, but whoever does not believe stands condemned already because he has not believed in the name of God's one and only Son. [19]This is the verdict: Light has come into the world, but men loved darkness instead of light because their deeds were evil. [20]Everyone who does evil hates the light, and will not come into the light for fear that his deeds will be exposed. [21]But whoever lives by the truth comes into the light, so that it may be seen plainly that what he has done has been done through God."

John 3 Chart

Causes	**Effects**

Genesis 3 (New King James Version)

1Now the serpent was more cunning than any beast of the field which the LORD God had
made. And he said to the woman, "Has God indeed said, 'You shall not eat of every tree of the
garden'?"

2And the woman said to the serpent, "We may eat the fruit of the trees of the garden; 3but of
the fruit of the tree which *is* in the midst of the garden, God has said, 'You shall not eat it, nor
shall you touch it, lest you die.'"

4Then the serpent said to the woman, "You will not surely die. 5For God knows that in the
day you eat of it your eyes will be opened, and you will be like God, knowing good and evil."

6So when the woman saw that the tree was good for food, that it was pleasant to the eyes, and
a tree desirable to make one wise, she took of its fruit and ate. She also gave to her husband with
her, and he ate. 7Then the eyes of both of them were opened, and they knew that they were
naked; and they sewed fig leaves together and made themselves coverings.

8And they heard the sound of the LORD God walking in the garden in the cool of the day, and
Adam and his wife hid themselves from the presence of the LORD God among the trees of the
garden.

9Then the LORD God called to Adam and said to him, "Where are you?"

10So he said, "I heard Your voice in the garden, and I was afraid because I was naked; and I
hid myself."

11 And He said, "Who told you that you were naked? Have you eaten from the tree of which I
commanded you that you should not eat?"

12 Then the man said, "The woman whom You gave to be with me, she gave me of the tree,
and I ate."

13 And the LORD God said to the woman, "What is this you have done?"

The woman said, "The serpent deceived me, and I ate."

14 So the LORD God said to the serpent: "Because you have done this, You are cursed more
than all cattle, and more than every beast of the field; on your belly you shall go, and you shall
eat dust all the days of your life. 15 And I will put enmity between you and the woman, and
between your seed and her Seed; He shall bruise your head, and you shall bruise His heel."

16 To the woman He said: "I will greatly multiply your sorrow and your conception; In pain
you shall bring forth children; Your desire shall be for your husband, and he shall rule over you."

17 Then to Adam He said, "Because you have heeded the voice of your wife, and have eaten
from the tree of which I commanded you, saying, 'You shall not eat of it': "Cursed is the ground
for your sake; In toil you shall eat of it all the days of your life. 18 Both thorns and thistles it shall
bring forth for you, and you shall eat the herb of the field. 19 In the sweat of your face you shall
eat bread till you return to the ground, for out of it you were taken; for dust you are, and to dust
you shall return."

20 And Adam called his wife's name Eve, because she was the mother of all living.

21 Also for Adam and his wife the LORD God made tunics of skin, and clothed them.

22 Then the LORD God said, "Behold, the man has become like one of Us, to know good and
evil. And now, lest he put out his hand and take also of the tree of life, and eat, and live
forever"—23 therefore the LORD God sent him out of the garden of Eden to till the ground from
which he was taken. 24 So He drove out the man; and He placed cherubim at the east of the

garden of Eden, and a flaming sword which turned every way, to guard the way to the tree of life.

Genesis 3 Chart

Causes	**Effects**
______________________________	______________________________

Romans 5 (Darby's New Translation[2])

1Therefore having been justified on the principle of faith, we have peace towards God
through our Lord Jesus Christ; 2by whom we have also access by faith into this favour in which
we stand, and we boast in hope of the glory of God.

3And not only [that], but we also boast in tribulations, knowing that tribulation works
endurance; 4and endurance, experience; and experience, hope; 5and hope does not make
ashamed, because the love of God is shed abroad in our hearts by [the] Holy Spirit which has
been given to us: 6for we being still without strength, in [the] due time Christ has died for [the]
ungodly. 7For scarcely for [the] just [man] will one die, for perhaps for [the] good [man] some
one might also dare to die; 8but God commends his love to us, in that, we being still sinners,
Christ has died for us. 9Much rather therefore, having been now justified in [the power of] his
blood, we shall be saved by him from wrath. 10For if, being enemies, we have been reconciled to
God through the death of his Son, much rather, having been reconciled, we shall be saved in [the
power of] his life.

11And not only [that], but [we are] making our boast in God, through our Lord Jesus Christ,
through whom now we have received the reconciliation. 12For this [cause], even as by one man

[2] This translation attempts to more literally follow the Greek and uses brackets to insert English words implied but not used in the original.

sin entered into the world, and by sin death; and thus death passed upon all men, for that all have sinned: 13(for until law sin was in [the] world; but sin is not put to account when there is no law; 14but death reigned from Adam until Moses, even upon those who had not sinned in the likeness of Adam's transgression, who is [the] figure of him to come. 15But [shall] not the act of favour [be] as the offence? For if by the offence of one the many have died, much rather has the grace of God, and the free gift in grace, which [is] by the one man Jesus Christ, abounded unto the many. 16And [shall] not as by one that has sinned [be] the gift? For the judgment [was] of one to condemnation, but the act of favour, of many offences unto justification. 17For if by the offence of the one death reigned by the one, much rather shall those who receive the abundance of grace, and of the free gift of righteousness, reign in life by the one Jesus Christ:) 18so then as [it was] by one offence towards all men to condemnation, so by one righteousness toward all men for justification of life. 19For as indeed by the disobedience of the one man the many have been constituted sinners, so also by the obedience of the one the many will be constituted righteous. 20But law came in, in order that the offence might abound; but where sin abounded grace has overabounded, 21in order that, even as sin has reigned in [the power of] death, so also grace might reign through righteousness to eternal life through Jesus Christ our Lord.

Romans 5 Chart

Causes	**Effects**
______________________________	______________________________

WRITING ASSIGNMENT

Select a topic on which to write a cause and effect argument. It should be related in some clear way to the papers written for previous assignments. The structure of this paper is what will make it unique. A successful cause and effect argument is one that meets this simple rule of logic: If A is true, then B is true. "If the soccer players don't drink enough water, they will get dehydrated." A biblical model comes from John 5:46 where Jesus says, "If you believed Moses, you would believe me, for he wrote about me." Another example is John 7:17 where Jesus says to some Jews at a feast, "If anyone chooses to do God's will, he will find out whether my teaching comes from God or whether I speak on my own."

1. Write a thesis statement in the form of cause and effect: If ____________________ is true, then ____________________ will be true. Writing this thesis statement may take some brainstorming. Consider the various causes and their effects as they apply to your area of interest. Identify one cause that particularly concerns you, and list the potential effects.

Cause	**Effects**
________________________________	____
	____
	____

Alternately, identify one effect that particularly interests you, and list the potential causes.

Causes	**Effect**
________________________________	____
________________________________	
________________________________	

2. Now sketch out in your journal or on computer some practice sentences and paragraphs indicating the way your paper is likely to develop.
3. With the brainstorming complete, it is time to do research to find out the validity of the cause and effect sequence you are exploring. To carry out your research, follow the "Research Using Bloom's Taxonomy" guidelines provided in Chapter 7. Assume that your professor

will require three literature reviews along with the final paper (show your work!). Be sure to accurately document sources according to guidelines in the *MLA Handbook*.

4. Normally it takes two or three pages to successfully explore and explain a cause and effect sequence to the satisfaction of the reader. When you have done this, and when your paper has been typed on computer in correct MLA format including an accurate Works Cited page, you are ready for a review of your paper by a peer.

(name of person writing review) ____________________________________

PEER REVIEW: Have a fellow student read and evaluate the cause and effect paper. The instructor is likely to assign partners for students who have just done the same exercise.

____ Make sure the final sentence of the introductory paragraph of a cause/effect paper clearly states a thesis in cause/effect structure. Example: "If the soccer players don't drink enough water, they will get dehydrated."

____ List below the causes and their effects explored in this paper.

Causes	**Effects**
________________________________	____
________________________________	____
________________________________	____

____ Make sure the writer has used clear and unambiguous language.

____ Evaluate the structure and confirm that each paragraph has only one central idea.

____ Delete unnecessary details.

____ Be sure all connections and transitions between sentences and paragraphs are effective.

____ Review the Works Cited page for accurate format based on the *MLA Handbook.*

____ List any relevant questions on the topic the author has failed to answer.

PLANNING THE REWRITE

In addition to carefully considering the suggestions of the peer review, see also the helpful suggestions on page 46 of the *MLA Handbook* on "Writing Drafts." Rewrite the cause and effect paper into a smooth-flowing and logical discourse that clearly shows the links between the various causes and effects you have identified.

CHAPTER 10: DEDUCTIVE ARGUMENT

The linear logic of cause/effect reasoning discussed in the previous chapter is characteristic of the Christian and Western tradition and is often required by college writing teachers: If A is true, then B is true. The next step for thinkers trained in linear logic is the syllogism, which adds one or more additional components. Writers become like detectives who realize it can be *deduced* that if A is true, and if B is true, then C is true. Example: "If all freshmen take tests, and if Caleb is a freshman, then Caleb will take tests." This is a syllogism.

The argument that can be reduced to a syllogism is a sound argument, and the writer who argues based on a syllogism is less likely to fall into logical fallacies. The Apostle Paul wrote in Romans 10:9, "If you confess with your mouth, 'Jesus is Lord,' and believe in your heart that God raised him from the dead, you will be saved." This concise statement reduces the message of the entire New Testament to a syllogism that would make sense for a Roman audience trained in the type of logic based on linear thinking:

If A is true: <u>if you confess with your mouth, "Jesus is Lord</u>"

And If B is true: <u>believe in your heart that God raised him from the dead</u>

Then C is true: <u>you will be saved</u>.

In this argument both conditions have to be true before the conclusion is true—it is a *conjunctive* argument. By contrast, a *disjunctive* argument would read, "If A is true, **or** if B is true, then C is true. The beauty of a syllogism is that it reduces an argument to its essence—very useful when trying to identify the exact thesis of a written argument.

The Apostle Paul's conjunctive syllogism targeted an audience that appreciated the linear logic taught by the Greek philosopher Socrates (469-399 BC), an early practitioner of logic admired by the Christian philosopher Augustin (AD 354-430), author of *City of God*:[1]

> Socrates … directed the entire effort of philosophy to the correction and regulation of manners, all who went before him having expended their greatest efforts in the investigation of physical, that is, natural phenomena…. For he saw … causes he believed to be ultimately reducible to nothing else than the will of the one true and supreme God,—[2]and on this account he thought they could only be comprehended by a purified mind; and therefore that all diligence ought to be given to the purification of the life by good morals, in order that the mind, delivered from the depressing weight of lusts, might raise itself upward by its native vigor to eternal things, and might, with purified understanding, contemplate that nature which is incorporeal and unchangeable light, where live the causes of all created natures. (145-146)

Plato (427-347 BC), a student of Socrates, is credited with combining the active and contemplative parts of philosophy and then reorganizing it into three parts. Augustin identifies the three parts as "the first moral, which is chiefly occupied with action; the second natural, of which the object is contemplation; and the third rational, which discriminates between the true and the false" (146). Christian philosophers appreciate Plato because he entertained this idea of

---

[1] This author is often spelled "Augustine," but not in this source.

[2] A comma followed by a dash (,—) is not correct MLA style, but it is a faithful reproduction of the original and therefore must be retained in the quote.

God: "In Him are to be found the cause of existence, the ultimate reason for the understanding, and the end in reference to which the whole life is to be regulated. Of which three things, the first is understood to pertain to the natural, the second to the rational, and the third to the moral part of philosophy" (Augustin 147).

Aristotle (384-322 BC) studied under Plato for 20 years and later applied his skills to the perfection of rhetoric in the form of his theory of the syllogism. A very basic introduction to Aristotelian logic appears below.

FROM SYLLOGISM TO SOUND ARGUMENT[3]

A logically *valid* syllogism is one in which the *reasoning* from premises to a conclusion is *accurate*:

All women are intelligent.

Kendra is a woman.

Therefore, Kendra is intelligent.

This argument is logically valid because the *reasoning* is accurate. That is, if the major and minor premises are true (the first and second sentences), then the conclusion also must be true. However, since it is not true that all women are intelligent, the major premise is false and therefore the conclusion must be false. **Insight:** *A valid syllogism can yield a false conclusion.*

Also be aware that the conclusion of a *valid* syllogism with false premises could still be true, but not because of the premises:

All Irishmen are aggressive.

Ivan is an Irishman.

Therefore, Ivan is aggressive.

---

[3] Information in this section is derived from Goodpaster 134-192.

The structure of the above syllogism is *valid*, but the first premise is obviously false.

Similarly, it is possible to have a syllogism that is not valid—the *reasoning* is inaccurate—even though it has true premises and even a true conclusion:

Some animals are brown.

All dogs are animals.

Therefore, some dogs are brown.

Each premise is true, and the conclusion is true, yet the syllogism is invalid—the conclusion cannot reasonably be derived from the premises.

Confusing causes with effects often results in syllogisms that are true but not valid. To say that "all freshmen take tests," and that "Tonya takes tests," therefore "Tonya is a freshman" is not valid because other people besides just freshmen take tests. Reversing the order results in a syllogism that is both valid and true:

All freshmen take tests.

Tonya is a freshman.

Therefore, Tonya takes tests.

Insight: The *validity* of an argument depends on its form, not on the truth of its premises. Consequently, an argument that depends on false premises could be valid, and an argument based on true premises could be invalid. Only premises and conclusions are *true* or *false*.

A sound argument is both *valid* and *true*. The goal of linear logic is to develop syllogisms that have both true premises and valid reasoning—this results in a sound *deductive* argument. This is the form used by many church fathers to structure persuasive theological arguments and is still respected today. Writing students who can reduce their argument to a thesis statement in the form of a syllogism have taken the first step to writing convincingly and persuasively using linear logic that will impress teachers from cultures shaped by Aristotelian logic.

No matter whether a writer uses deductive argument described here or the inductive argument form discussed in the next chapter, it is vital to avoid the errors in reasoning that crop up in every culture and system of logic. These errors are known as logical fallacies, and writers who commit them destroy their own credibility and fail to persuade.

LOGICAL FALLACIES

A logical fallacy is an error in reasoning. Dr. Michael C. Labossiere has identified 42 such fallacies (see http://www.nizkor.org/features/fallacies/), and an internet search will turn up many different names for the same reasoning errors. A shorter list is provided here of the more common types:

A **hasty generalization** occurs when a writer draws a conclusion based on too little evidence: "Look at the damage those skateboarders are doing to the park bench. All those 'sidewalk surfers' are destructive."

Assignment: Write down a similar example common in your experience:

____

____

Similarly, the **stereotype** ascribes a common group trait to an individual: "He's a university student—he must be brilliant." Usually stereotypes are negative, as in, "Oh, he's from Subterranea, and all Subterraneans are lazy."

Assignment: Write down a similar example common in your experience:

____

____

An **appeal to the crowd** argument uses irrational fears and prejudices to persuade: "If we buy oil from Russia, those Communists will take over the world using our money!"

Assignment: Write down a similar example common in your experience:

____

____

A **non sequitur** (Latin for "it does not follow") draws unwarranted conclusions from irrelevant evidence: "Tony really chews through the groceries. Some day he'll be seriously overweight."

Assignment: Write down a similar example common in your experience:

____

____

The **either/or** fallacy presumes that only two choices exist when actually there are many alternatives: "Unless we find a cure for AIDS, the human race will be wiped out."

Assignment: Write down a similar example common in your experience:

____

____

Begging the question, or "petitio principii" (Latin), refers to an issue in a formal debate that one side may ask the other side to concede in order to speed up the proceedings. But such a statement is illegitimate because it argues for the truth of an unproven statement: "Because the higher speed limit is responsible for so many deaths, it should be reduced."

Assignment: Write down a similar example common in your experience:

____

____

A **circular argument** uses repetition to replace proofs: "That painting is the most beautiful art in the room because it is better than the others."

Assignment: Write down a similar example common in your experience:

____

____

Arguing off the point ignores the question by introducing irrelevant material and redirecting the debate. This technique is routinely practiced by politicians. When asked, "What will you do to reduce crime in the neighborhood?" they are likely to say, "Our police force is underpaid and overworked, which is exasperated by the deterioration of the nuclear family, and the current administration is more concerned about what roads to pave than about how to make those very roads safe to drive down."

Assignment: Write down a similar example common in your experience:

____

____

The **ad hominem** (Latin for "to the man") argument attacks the individual rather than addressing the issue: "Professor Gibson doesn't deserve a promotion to the next faculty rank. He's always writing letters to the editor and he has a troubled marriage." This attack ignores the issue of whether Gibson deserves a promotion based on his job performance.

Assignment: Write down a similar example common in your experience:

____

____

The **faulty analogy** assumes that two things are similar when in fact they are not: "If America can land a person on the moon and bring him safely back to earth, certainly we can solve the problem of global warming."

Assignment: Write down a similar example common in your experience:

____

____

Post hoc, ergo propter hoc (Latin for "after this, therefore because of this") refers to an error in cause and effect reasoning (see previous chapter for discussion of cause and effect).

Assignment: Write down a similar example common in your experience:

____

____

Internet Assignment: Type "logical fallacy" in the space provided on your internet search engine and visit five websites that discuss these issues. Make a chart like the one illustrated below and summarize the most important thing you learn by visiting each of the five sites.

Website 1: ________________________ What I learned: ________________________

Website 2: ________________________ What I learned: ________________________

Website 3: ________________________ What I learned: ________________________

Website 4: ________________________ What I learned: ________________________

Website 5: ________________________ What I learned: ________________________

PRE-WRITING ASSIGNMENT

What is an important argument in your area of interest that particularly fascinates you? Just as the Apostle Paul faced the pressing issues of explaining the good news about Jesus to a skeptical audience, so you will find it necessary to argue convincingly for something vital in your academic field. Writing such an argument will draw on all the work you have done throughout this text, and will also require additional research. It is likely that your instructor will require an argument of at least six to eight pages of careful reasoning.

Topic of interest: ____

Vital issue within topic: ____

Common questions about the issue:

1. ____

2. ____

3. ____

4. ____

5. ____

Possible answers to the questions:

1. ____

2. ____

3. ____

4. ____

5. ____

A: Your instructor may give you a choice of using either deductive reasoning (the subject of this chapter) or inductive reasoning (the subject of the next chapter). If you plan to use deductive reasoning, make a syllogism out of the above information:

If A is true: ____

and If B is true: ____

Then C is true: ____

B: If you plan to use inductive reasoning, review the summary of the Scientific Method in Chapter 3 and the discussion of inductive argument in the next chapter. Next, make a list of the evidence you will need to collect, the sources of persuasive stories and information, and the steps you will need to follow in order to make your argument plausible and convincing.

Thought: The goal of *deductive* argument is often to achieve a "proof" that cannot be denied; the goal of an *inductive* argument is often to provide compelling evidence that a given point of view is reasonable and plausible.

DEDUCTIVE MODEL

Before exploring a sample deductive argument from the Bible, an important distinction must be made between the approach of theologians and literary critics. Leland Ryken notes that while biblical scholars tend to explore the text in a fragmented, line-by-line analysis that leans heavily on deductive reasoning, literary critics use more inductive reasoning by asking such questions as these: "How is the story structured? What are the unifying narrative principles? … How does the story unfold sequentially? …What are the plot conflicts, and how are they resolved? How does the protagonist develop as the story progresses? … How is the thematic meaning of the story embodied in narrative form?" (28) Ryken notes that while literary criticism and biblical scholarship are complementary, they are vastly different and have different objectives.

Some authors such as the seventeenth-century writer John Bunyan used both methods. As a preacher he used linear logic as he expounded line by line, precept upon precept, on individual texts. But he also had the capacity, as Ryken describes it, to "respond with a child's sense of wonder to story, to sensations, to the weather, to elemental emotions such as terror or love or trust, to mystery, to miracle" (29).

Not all theologians bury themselves in the details. Inductive Bible study presents a way for theologians to read scripture as literature—far different from the systematic theology of a John Calvin, but natural to the informally educated like John Bunyan who tended to read scripture in a literal sense as *story*. The distinction is profound. Calvin's systematic theology leaned heavily on deductive argument in which the conclusion must be true if the premises are true. When the conclusion does not necessarily follow from the premises, a deductive argument is invalid. But the scriptures tell a story that is often more easily approached inductively by looking at what really happened as opposed to what should have happened based on the evidence. See Chapter 11 to explore the inductive approach in more detail.

Deductive Reasoning: Acts 6:8-7:60 (New Revised Standard Version)

[8]Stephen, full of grace and power, did great wonders and signs among the people. [9]Then some of those who belonged to the synagogue of the Freedmen (as it was called), Cyrenians, Alexandrians, and others of those from Cilicia and Asia, stood up and argued with Stephen. [10]But they could not withstand the wisdom and the Spirit with which he spoke. [11]Then they secretly instigated some men to say, "We have heard him speak blasphemous words against Moses and God." [12]They stirred up the people as well as the elders and the scribes; then they suddenly confronted him, seized him, and brought him before the council. [13]They set up false witnesses who said, "This man never stops saying things against this holy place and the law; [14]for we have heard him say that this Jesus of Nazareth will destroy this place and will change the customs that Moses handed on to us." [15]And all who sat in the council looked intently at him, and they saw that his face was like the face of an angel.

Acts 7: [1]Then the high priest asked him, "Are these things so?" [2]And Stephen replied:

"Brothers and fathers, listen to me. The God of glory appeared to our ancestor Abraham when he was in Mesopotamia, before he lived in Haran, [3]and said to him, 'Leave your country and your relatives and go to the land that I will show you.' [4]Then he left the country of the Chaldeans and settled in Haran. After his father died, God had him move from there to this country in which you are now living. [5]He did not give him any of it as a heritage, not even a foot's length, but promised to give it to him as his possession and to his descendants after him, even though he had no child. [6]And God spoke in these terms, that his descendants would be resident aliens in a country belonging to others, who would enslave them and mistreat them during four hundred years. [7]'But I will judge the nation that they serve,' said God, 'and after that they shall come out and worship me in this place.' [8]Then he gave him the covenant of circumcision. And so Abraham became the father of Isaac and circumcised him on the eighth day; and Isaac became the father of Jacob, and Jacob of the twelve patriarchs.

[9]"The patriarchs, jealous of Joseph, sold him into Egypt; but God was with him, [10]and rescued him from all his afflictions, and enabled him to win favor and to show wisdom when he stood before Pharaoh, king of Egypt, who appointed him ruler over Egypt and over all his household. [11]Now there came a famine throughout Egypt and Canaan, and great suffering, and our ancestors could find no food. [12]But when Jacob heard that there was grain in Egypt, he sent our ancestors there on their first visit. [13]On the second visit Joseph made himself known to his brothers, and Joseph's family became known to Pharaoh. [14]Then Joseph sent and invited his father Jacob and all his relatives to come to him, seventy-five in all; [15]so Jacob went down to Egypt. He himself died there as well as our ancestors, [16]and their bodies were brought back to Shechem and laid in the tomb that Abraham had bought for a sum of silver from the sons of Hamor in Shechem.

[17]"But as the time drew near for the fulfillment of the promise that God had made to Abraham, our people in Egypt increased and multiplied [18]until another king who had not known Joseph ruled over Egypt. [19]He dealt craftily with our race and forced our ancestors to abandon their infants so that they would die. [20]At this time Moses was born, and he was beautiful before God. For three months he was brought up in his father's house; [21]and when he was abandoned, Pharaoh's daughter adopted him and brought him up as her own son. [22]So Moses was instructed in all the wisdom of the Egyptians and was powerful in his words and deeds.

[23]"When he was forty years old, it came into his heart to visit his relatives, the Israelites. [24]When he saw one of them being wronged, he defended the oppressed man and avenged him by striking down the Egyptian. [25]He supposed that his kinsfolk would understand that God through him was rescuing them, but they did not understand. [26]The next day he came to some of them as they were quarreling and tried to reconcile them, saying, 'Men, you are brothers; why do you wrong each other?' [27]But the man who was wronging his neighbor pushed Moses aside, saying, 'Who made you a ruler and a judge over us? [28]Do you want to kill me as you killed the Egyptian yesterday?' [29]When he heard this, Moses fled and became a resident alien in the land of Midian. There he became the father of two sons.

[30]"Now when forty years had passed, an angel appeared to him in the wilderness of Mount Sinai, in the flame of a burning bush. [31]When Moses saw it, he was amazed at the sight; and as he approached to look, there came the voice of the Lord: [32]'I am the God of your ancestors, the God of Abraham, Isaac, and Jacob.' Moses began to tremble and did not dare to look. [33]Then the Lord said to him, 'Take off the sandals from your feet, for the place where you are standing is holy ground. [34]I have surely seen the mistreatment of my people who are in Egypt and have

heard their groaning, and I have come down to rescue them. Come now, I will send you to Egypt.'

35"It was this Moses whom they rejected when they said, 'Who made you a ruler and a judge?' and whom God now sent as both ruler and liberator through the angel who appeared to him in the bush. 36He led them out, having performed wonders and signs in Egypt, at the Red Sea, and in the wilderness for forty years. 37This is the Moses who said to the Israelites, 'God will raise up a prophet for you from your own people as he raised me up.' 38He is the one who was in the congregation in the wilderness with the angel who spoke to him at Mount Sinai, and with our ancestors; and he received living oracles to give to us. 39Our ancestors were unwilling to obey him; instead, they pushed him aside, and in their hearts they turned back to Egypt, 40saying to Aaron, 'Make gods for us who will lead the way for us; as for this Moses who led us out from the land of Egypt, we do not know what has happened to him.' 41At that time they made a calf, offered a sacrifice to the idol, and reveled in the works of their hands. 42But God turned away from them and handed them over to worship the host of heaven, as it is written in the book of the prophets: 'Did you offer to me slain victims and sacrifices forty years in the wilderness, O house of Israel? 43No; you took along the tent of Moloch, and the star of your god Rephan, the images that you made to worship; so I will remove you beyond Babylon.'

44"Our ancestors had the tent of testimony in the wilderness, as God directed when he spoke to Moses, ordering him to make it according to the pattern he had seen. 45Our ancestors in turn brought it in with Joshua when they dispossessed the nations that God drove out before our ancestors. And it was there until the time of David, 46who found favor with God and asked that he might find a dwelling place for the house of Jacob. 47But it was Solomon who built a house for him. 48Yet the Most High does not dwell in houses made with human hands; as the prophet

says, 49 ‘Heaven is my throne, and the earth is my footstool. What kind of house will you build
for me, says the Lord, or what is the place of my rest? 50 Did not my hand make all these things?’

51 "You stiff-necked people, uncircumcised in heart and ears, you are forever opposing the
Holy Spirit, just as your ancestors used to do. 52 Which of the prophets did your ancestors not
persecute? They killed those who foretold the coming of the Righteous One, and now you have
become his betrayers and murderers. 53 You are the ones that received the law as ordained by
angels, and yet you have not kept it."

54 When they heard these things, they became enraged and ground their teeth at Stephen.
55 But filled with the Holy Spirit, he gazed into heaven and saw the glory of God and Jesus
standing at the right hand of God. 56 "Look," he said, "I see the heavens opened and the Son of
Man standing at the right hand of God!" 57 But they covered their ears, and with a loud shout all
rushed together against him. 58 Then they dragged him out of the city and began to stone him; and
the witnesses laid their coats at the feet of a young man named Saul. 59 While they were stoning
Stephen, he prayed, "Lord Jesus, receive my spirit." 60 Then he knelt down and cried out in a loud
voice, "Lord, do not hold this sin against them." When he had said this, he died.

ANALYSIS QUESTIONS

1. Identify the deductions reached by Stephen's audience as a result of hearing his argument.
2. How do their deductions differ from those Stephen has reached?
3. Discuss how it is possible that two people hearing the same evidence can reach opposite conclusions.
4. Explore in writing the author’s purpose in narrating the story of Stephen. What is he trying to teach his audience? What, if anything, is he trying to teach you?

5. Showing action is an important part of many arguments. In your opinion, what is the most exciting action that takes place in this story? Why do you like it?
6. Identify the main conflict surrounding this argument. Be specific about the details.
7. How does conflict make the argument more interesting?
8. From what point of view is this argument presented? How would the argument feel differently if it were told from the point of view of the high priest?
9. Stephen's argument, a narrative within a narrative, is used in this story to reveal character. In what ways do you feel you know Stephen the human being as well as Stephen the servant of Jesus better because you have "heard" him work his way methodically through an argument?
10. What argument techniques of Stephen's can you borrow to enhance the quality of the argument you will write?

SAMPLE ARGUMENT

Students often find this writing assignment the most difficult of all. Therefore, a sample of the kind of systematic thinking necessary in deductive reasoning is provided below. Charles White, Professor of Christian Thought and History at Spring Arbor University, is a graduate of Harvard College (BA) and Boston University (MA, Ph.D.). This essay is the condensed introduction to a much longer essay.

Dr. White argues, (A) if we are to love God with our minds, and (B) if we are to give an answer for the hope that is in us, and (C) if our actions depend on our beliefs, then (D) we need systematic theology. No doubt many students reading this text believe themselves to have no interest in systematic theology, a concept they may not understand, perhaps haven't read about before, and have no idea that it might be valuable to them personally. The objective in reading this argument is to see whether these views change—to see whether the argument succeeds. And if it does, then the powers of persuasion are shown to be very useful indeed, and these same students might well feel motivated to master the art of deductive reasoning and writing.

The Puzzle of Systematic Theology

By Charles Edward White

How can Christians worship God the Father, God the Son, and God the Holy Spirit and still say there is only one God? How can Jesus be both man and God at the same time? How can God be all-powerful and all-wise and still let there be so much undeserved suffering in the world? What happens to the people who die without ever having a chance to have faith in Christ? Can true believers lose their salvation? Or as the title of a book for teenagers asks, "If God loves me, why can't I get my locker open?"

These questions are just a few of the infinite number of theological questions the Bible never answers directly. There are thousands of subjects, ranging from the composition of the Godhead to the perseverance of the saints, which people wonder about, but find no definitive word from God. Yet if we are to love the Lord with our mind, as well as our heart, soul, and strength, we cannot ignore everything the Lord has not revealed. Further, if we are to give an answer for the hope that is in us, we need to make sure that our answer makes sense. In addition, if we are to be adult in our understanding, we must see the implications of what the Lord has told us. Only the very young need specific rules for every circumstance; with maturity comes the ability to apply general principles to various situations. Finally, because our actions often depend on our beliefs, those beliefs must be correct. Paul rebukes the Corinthians for letting a mistaken theology of the resurrection lead them into personal sin. Thus we all need systematic theology.

Systematic theology attempts to answer the questions God never addresses in the Bible. It aims to show how the various truths he has revealed relate to each other and to fill in the gaps between those revelations. It seeks to understand all the implications of what God has said and to fit everything he has revealed into a coherent pattern. Just as a scientist seeks to understand the world by discovering the laws that explain the various phenomena of nature, so the systematic theologian looks for the fundamental principles that underlie all that God has revealed in Scripture.

But natural laws are not part of nature: They are human inferences based on observed data. Like everything human, our understanding of natural laws can be improved. Ptolemy observed the night sky and announced the law that every heavenly body moves in a circle around the earth. Copernicus observed the sky more closely and modified the law by saying that the planets move in a circle around the sun. Later Newton made still more observations and developed the law of universal gravitation stating that every heavenly body attracts every other one. In our century Einstein showed that the laws Newton identified apply to everything we can see, and currently scientists are trying to formulate one law, a "unified field theory," that will describe the behavior of atoms as well as nebula. Human science is subject to constant improvement.

Similarly, systematic theology is not part of God's revelation: It is human reasoning based on God's truth. Like natural science, it can be improved. In the third century Sabellius based his theology on the Scriptures that teach God's unity. A century later Arius likewise firmly grasped half of the truth, emphasizing those verses that teach the subordination of the Son to the Father. It was not until Nicea that the church developed a theology that affirms both these truths. On some questions the mind of the church is settled: The idea of the Trinity is the standard of orthodoxy. In other areas, however, the discussion still goes on. Christians are still struggling to reconcile the seemingly divergent teachings of the Bible and to formulate in one coherent pattern all the Scripture teaches.

The struggle to develop a unified field theory that will explain all the Bible's teaching is a little bit like putting an old jigsaw puzzle together. Almost everyone has an old jigsaw puzzle around the house, but it is usually not in top condition. Often a few pieces get lost and sometimes even the original box comes up missing. Deprived of the picture of the finished puzzle to guide them and lacking some of the original pieces, puzzle workers have to rely on the shapes and colors of the remaining pieces for clues to the pattern of the puzzle. With a thirty-piece puzzle designed for a toddler reconstructing the puzzle is an easy task, but with a thousand-piece monster it is almost impossible. Is it any wonder people have trouble fitting the 31,145 verses of the Bible into a systematic pattern?

People have trouble doing systematic theology because not all the pieces they want are there. The Bible clearly teaches that God is absolutely sovereign: That is one piece we must fit in. But the Bible just as clearly teaches that humans are free and responsible for their actions. That is another piece of the puzzle. Unfortunately for us, the pieces that connect God's sovereignty and human freedom are missing from the Bible. Given the pieces we have to work with, there is no way we can fit them together.

Besides not having all the pieces we want, a bigger problem with the puzzle of theology is that we do not have the box with the picture to show us what the finished puzzle looks like. Which pieces go in the center and which go on the edge? Do the pieces with one flat side make the border as one would expect or is this a very sophisticated puzzle with an irregular border and four flat matching quarters coming together in the middle?

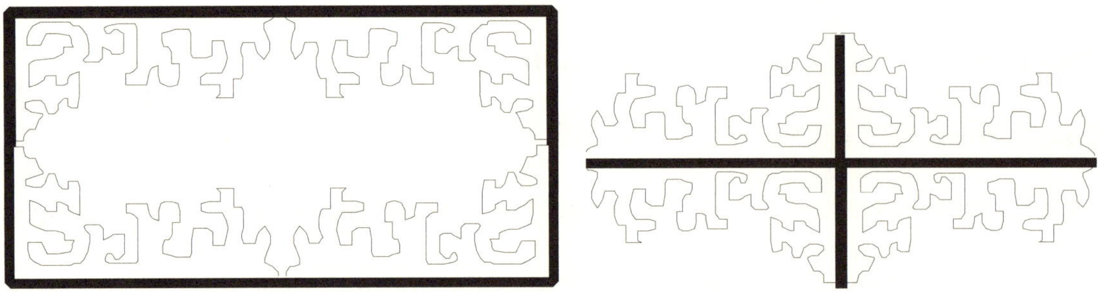

Faced with the problem of putting together an old jigsaw puzzle, people have to adopt certain rules. First, they must use every piece of the puzzle. They will never reconstruct the original if they simply throw away the pieces they find hard to fit. Second, they must not cut or modify any piece of the puzzle. Cutting off a knob from one piece is not the correct way to make it fit with another. Third, they are allowed to construct new pieces to fill in the gaps between the old pieces. This process is simply replacing what has been lost. Finally, the finished work must display a picture of something. After all, the challenge of a jigsaw puzzle is reconstructing the picture that has been taken apart.

The rules that apply to old jigsaw puzzles also apply to systematic theology. First, use every piece of the puzzle. We cannot simply ignore the Scripture's teaching about hell because we do not like it. All scripture is profitable for doctrine so we must not throw any of it away. Next, we must not cut the pieces we are given. The Jesus-pieces we find in Scripture contain more statements about God's judgment than about his love. We cannot trim away the harsh words to make the pieces fit into a portrait of Jesus meek and mild. We can, however, construct new pieces to make the original ones fit together. The doctrine of the Trinity is an obvious example. Though nowhere taught in Scripture, it holds together the Scripture's teaching of the unity and diversity in the Godhead. Our final job as systematic theologians is to construct a picture that makes sense. Some ideas are central, while others are peripheral. We must determine the organizing themes of Scripture and fit all the other ideas into their pattern.

It is in this final area that systematicians will have the most disagreement. Just as puzzle makers might disagree about whether they are putting together the picture of a horse or a dog, so theologians working on the soteriology section of the puzzle will disagree about what is central in the Bible's doctrine of our salvation. Although Calvin himself did not do so, some of his followers see the sovereignty of God as the central fact in human salvation. They speak much about God's power, his grace for the elect, and the efficacy of his decrees, but do not say much about how his actions are loving or just to the reprobate whom he elected for damnation before the foundation of the world. Thus when they assemble this section of the puzzle of theology, they see a huge throne in the center and little hearts out on the edge. Others argue that the central picture is really a cross, and that God's love and justice shape all the Bible's teaching about our salvation. For them God's sovereignty is present in the picture, but it is way out on the border of their thought.

It may be that someone will devise a way to put this section of the puzzle together that does equal justice to God's sovereignty, love, and justice. This formulation will eventually win the approbation of the whole church the way the thought of Athanasius enlightened the early Christians about the Trinity. We should be thankful that earlier thinkers have done so much of the work for us. When we approach the puzzle today we find that the first seven ecumenical councils put together some of the pieces to produce coherent pictures of the Godhead and of Christ. Our job is to put together the rest including the sections on pneumatology, soteriology, anthropology, and ecclesiology. Someday we may all agree on how it all fits together, but probably we will keep working on it until the puzzle maker himself returns and shows us where everything belongs.

ANALYSIS QUESTIONS

11. In what ways did the author's logical thinking process make it easier to follow the argument?
12. What did you learn about the assumptions behind systematic theology that you had not considered before?
13. Dr. White's essay is an argument by analogy. How effective was the analogy in helping you understand, accept, and appreciate his argument?
14. Which of Dr. White's argument methods will you consider using to make your own argument more persuasive?

WRITING ASSIGNMENT

Review the notes written in the pre-writing section of this chapter, then begin writing your own argument. Again, the topic you select should be related in some way to the papers you have previously written and should have a useful application to your major field of study in college. Put the paper in standard MLA format including footnotes and a Works Cited page. The instructor will tell you the required length. When writing a deductive argument, it is vital to follow a deliberate logical structure. The format below is strongly recommended:

Introductory Paragraph: Use several introductory sentences to explain the issue, why it is important, and how it will be approached. Even if this is not a deductive argument, this paragraph should *contain the essence* of the syllogism developed earlier. If the argument *is* deductive, this thesis should be written *in the form* of a logical syllogism. This introduction can be up to half a page in length.

Supporting Argument One: Most arguments have a minimum of three supporting arguments, all of which have been outlined and summarized in the first paragraph. The first supporting argument can be from several paragraphs to several pages.

Supporting Argument Two: The second supporting argument and is likely to be of approximately the same length as the previous section.

Supporting Argument Three: This section contains the third supporting argument. Additional supporting arguments may be included as necessary.

Conclusion: The conclusion reviews, summarizes, and clenches the argument presented in the preceding pages.

ANALYZING AN ARGUMENT

To carry out your research, follow the "Research Using Bloom's Taxonomy" guidelines provided in Chapter 7. The professor will tell you how many literature reviews are required. As you transfer information from your literature reviews into the argument paper, be sure to avoid plagiarism by accurately identifying sources, using parenthetical references correctly, and including each source in the Works Cited. Make sure to carefully follow all formatting and punctuation guidelines provided in the *MLA Handbook.*

As you study the various publications that will serve as sources for your literature reviews, notice that authors frequently make a case for some action or interpretation of events by presenting claims backed by reasons and evidence. Examine the logical soundness of the author's case by evaluating the line of reasoning and the use of evidence.

1. Ask what is claimed.
    a. Figure out what that claim assumes. Are the assumptions stated or unstated?
    b. Ferret out the logical fallacies if you can identify any.

c. Discover what is offered as evidence, support, or proof.

d. Examine what is explicitly stated, claimed, or concluded.

e. Look for what is not stated but necessarily follows from what is stated.

2. Think of an alternative explanation and counter-examples.
3. Consider additional evidence that might weaken or strengthen the claims.
4. Determine what changes in the argument would make the reasoning more convincing.
5. Evaluate each source using the above guidelines. This will help you detect flawed arguments, select the best material, and develop your paper in a convincing way.

(name of person writing review) ________________________________

PEER REVIEW: Have a fellow student read and evaluate the argument paper, preferably someone who has also written an argument paper in the same format.

An argument usually expresses an assertion **(thesis)** about a **subject** to an **audience** for a particular reason **(purpose)**. Read the student argument and answer these questions:

1. Is the argument deductive or inductive? (See Chapter 11 about inductive arguments to understand the difference). If inductive, the thesis should summarize the scope of the investigation; if deductive, the thesis should resemble the form of a logical syllogism.
2. **Subject:** What is this essay about?

____

____

3. **Thesis:** What particular point is the author trying to make about this subject?

____

____

4. **Audience:** To whom is the author writing? How does its intended audience help shape the essay and influence its language and style?

____

____

5. **Purpose:** Why is the author writing this? To entertain? To inform? To persuade?

____

____

6. Evaluate the material based on the criteria outlined by Michael Osborn in Chapter 11. Both deductive and inductive arguments have the potential to achieve these criteria:

A How effective is this material in the elevation of the mind?

____

____

B Superior structure: Evaluate the structure to determine how superior it is.

____

____

C Bold imagery: What imagery does the author use, and how bold is it?

____

____

D What great challenge does the writer place before his readers?

____

____

E To what extent do you experience transport from reading this? Why?

____

____

7. Aristotle presents three argument strategies: *Ethos* (ethical appeal), *Pathos* (emotional appeal), and *Logos* (rational appeal). Next to each paragraph, identify which strategy is being used and how effective it is.

8. How successfully does this argument mix the writing strategies taught in previous chapters (narrative, description, process, definition, illustration, classification, comparison)? Try to identify places where one or more of these strategies could be used to strengthen the argument.

PLANNING THE REWRITE

A: Locate one of the most influential arguments in your field of study and write down the author, title, and other needed details for your Works Cited.

B: Evaluate that material based on the criteria outlined by Michael Osborn:

1. How effective is this material in the elevation of the mind?
2. Superior structure: Evaluate the structure to determine how superior it is.
3. Bold imagery: What imagery does the author use, and how bold is it?
4. What great challenge does the writer place before his readers?
5. To what extent do you experience transport from reading this? Why?

C. Give the main reasons why you think the argument identified above has influence in your field of study.

D: Evaluate the first draft of your own argument using the above criteria, then rewrite it based on your own critique as well as the input from your classmate's peer review.

CHAPTER 11: INDUCTIVE ARGUMENT

Inductive argument does not rely on the logical syllogisms and absolute proofs of deductive argument. Rather, it relies on accumulated evidence to infer strong probabilities. Example: “If the refrigerator is not running and the milk, butter, and cheese are spoiled, then the meat is probably rotten as well.” There is no direct relationship between the dairy products and the meat. There is no precise cause and effect. There is just that uneasy feeling that things kept in refrigerators don’t keep so well without *refrigeration.* There is also that horrible smell….

Inductive argument is both more ancient and more recent than deductive argument. Augustin writes that all the philosophers before Socrates "expended their greatest efforts in the investigation of physical, that is, natural phenomena" (145). This study of natural phenomena was revived a thousand years later when the English philosopher Francis Bacon (1561-1626) developed an experimental or inductive system of thinking known today as the Scientific Method.[1] Bacon's *Novum Organum* (*New Instrument of Learning*) proposed replacing Aristotle's logic with inductive reasoning based on raw evidence found in nature.

Inductive reasoning results in plausible theories as opposed to proven facts. When proof is not possible, it is reasonable to adopt the more modest goal of proposing a conclusion that is *probably* true. If the same experiment is conducted 100 times and the results are always the same, the result will *probably* be the same on the 101st try—but there are no guarantees! Much of

[1] See Chapter 3, "The Scientific Method" for a summary of this system of organizing and conducting an experiment.

the reasoning people do in everyday life is inductive—it produces *probable* conclusions rather than definite ones. Physicians accurately guess at the probable cause of a patient's symptoms without a definitive diagnosis. "I've seen 300 cases with these symptoms this month," they may say. "The prescription drug XYZ has cured everybody else—maybe it'll work for you…." Similarly, legal scholars frequently use inductive methods to determine what law governs a particular case, and journalists write editorials that lead to probable conclusions. All of them reach "reasonable" conclusions, and such reasoning pervades world cultures.

Inductive reasoning appeals to the creative side of the brain as opposed to the analytical side. Consider this example:

MONKEY HEART

Once upon a time, along a large river in Africa, there was a tree. In the tree lived a monkey. In the water beneath the tree a crocodile slept away the lazy days and dreamed about how delicious it would be to have a monkey sandwich. But he couldn't climb trees, so he thought hard about what to do. One day he said to the monkey, "We both have a friend on the other side of the river. He needs our help. How about if you and I go over there and help him?"

"But I can't swim across the river," said the monkey. "You will have to go alone."

"It is not suitable for me to go alone," he replied. "I will swim across the river and you can ride on my back."

Crocodiles are *good swimmers*, the monkey thought. Finally he said, "Okay, that is a good plan," and the monkey dropped down on the crocodile's back.

They started out, and when they got half way across the rushing water the crocodile said, "Oh! There is one thing I forgot to tell you."

"What is that?"

"Well, there is only one thing that can help our friend, and that is the heart of a monkey."

This news distressed the monkey. He looked back and saw it was a long way to the safety of his tree. He ran up and down, up and down the back of the crocodile, wondering what to do. Then, in a flash of inspiration, he ran to the head of the crocodile and spoke directly into its ear. "Oh dear," said the monkey. "We have a terrible problem!"

"And what might that be?" grinned the crocodile.

"I forgot to tell you—I have left my heart back there in my tree!"

"Is that so?" asked the surprised crocodile.

"Oh yes indeed! We monkeys never travel with our hearts. We must go back and get it."

The disappointed crocodile made a U-turn and swam under a low branch of the tree. The monkey leaped for the branch and scrambled up. Safely away, he called down to the crocodile, "I have found my heart, but I have also changed my mind. I think I'll just stay up here in my tree, where my heart is" (Bates 146-147).

It is possible to reduce an inductive argument to a syllogism, such as, "If you guard your heart, and if you do not listen to lies, then you will be safe." However, such an argument may not be as compelling as the story itself. And there are cultural reasons to avoid stating a case using linear logic. Satoshi Ishii writes that in Japan it is considered rude to make a clear and direct point. The accepted practice is to delicately imply a conclusion after carefully approaching the issue from several angles. In Ishii's culture there is no equivalent to thesis statements and topic sentences (97-102). Unfortunately, “foreign” students who fail to start with a thesis followed by "logical" points and a precise conclusion often receive worse grades than they deserve from teachers who do not recognize the structures of inductive arguments.

Inductive logic has its own structure and may be envisioned in many ways. Duane Elmer describes typical African preaching as a daisy-shaped presentation in which the speaker continually loops back to a central point after each story, illustration, or scripture reading. The strength of the argument builds each time the speaker reiterates the central point. Elmer writes, "There is something amazingly effective about this speaking style.... I benefited more from this circular, flower petal style than from many of the linear sermons" (156). This pattern turns up in the "I Have a Dream" speech by Martin Luther King, Jr. that appears later in this chapter.

ANTHANASIUS THE GREAT

The inductive approach to argument can be traced back to St. Anthanasius the Great (AD 251-356), an Egyptian monk who established a monastery near Alexandria. His advice was prized, most famously by Constantine Augustus and his sons, Constantius Augustus and Constans Augustus. Anthanasius advised the Greeks, "You lean on sophistical debates; and yet your monstrous idols are coming to naught, while our faith is spreading everywhere" (101). His disdain for deductive logic comes through when he quips, "You with your syllogisms and sophisms do not draw any [converts] from Christianity to Hellenism; we, teaching faith in Christ, despoil your superstition." Anthanasius then cast out the demons from some people standing there, "and the so-called philosophers were astonished and really stupefied at his wisdom and at the miracle that was done" (101-102).

Anthanasius taught that those who have faith in Christ "will no longer seek proofs by reasonings, but will think faith in Christ sufficient by itself" (104). He argues, "We win men by faith, which lays hold of real things before argument can logically establish them" (103). He reasons that knowledge about God must begin with faith: "Faith comes from the very build of the soul; but the art of logic from the skill of those who framed it. It follows that, to those who have an active belief, reasoned proofs are needless and probably useless. For what we know by faith, that you are trying to establish by argument. And often you cannot even put in words what we know; so that the action of faith is better and surer than your sophist's proofs" (101).

Anthanasius does not discredit the value of deductive logic in some circumstances. His point is that inductive reasoning has validity in matters of faith. The inductive approach provides a way to set aside personal prejudice and to see the Scriptures as God's story of his own active involvement in history. In essence, the inductive approach relies on what Beth Lynch calls "a willingness to 'experience' the text." She references Keats' concept of "negative capability" to experience uncertainty, mystery, and doubt without reaching after fact and reason (45). Asaph demonstrates this capacity in the passage below.

INDUCTIVE MODELS

Psalm 74 (NIV) An Argument with God in the form of a maskil of Asaph

1 Why have you rejected us forever, O God? Why does your anger smolder against the
sheep of your pasture? 2 Remember the people you purchased of old, the tribe of your
inheritance, whom you redeemed—Mount Zion, where you dwelt. 3 Turn your steps toward these
everlasting ruins, all this destruction the enemy has brought on the sanctuary.

4 Your foes roared in the place where you met with us; they set up their standards as
signs. 5 They behaved like men wielding axes to cut through a thicket of trees. 6 They smashed
all the carved paneling with their axes and hatchets. 7 They burned your sanctuary to the ground;
they defiled the dwelling place of your Name. 8 They said in their hearts, "We will crush them
completely!" They burned every place where God was worshiped in the land. 9 We are given no
miraculous signs; no prophets are left, and none of us knows how long this will be.

10 How long will the enemy mock you, O God? Will the foe revile your name forever?
11 Why do you hold back your hand, your right hand? Take it from the folds of your garment and
destroy them!

12 But you, O God, are my king from of old; you bring salvation upon the earth. 13 It
was you who split open the sea by your power; you broke the heads of the monster in the waters.

14 It was you who crushed the heads of Leviathan and gave him as food to the creatures of the
desert. 15 It was you who opened up springs and streams; you dried up the ever flowing rivers. 16
The day is yours, and yours also the night; you established the sun and moon. 17 It was you who
set all the boundaries of the earth; you made both summer and winter.

18 Remember how the enemy has mocked you, O LORD, how foolish people have
reviled your name. 19 Do not hand over the life of your dove to wild beasts; do not forget the
lives of your afflicted people forever. 20 Have regard for your covenant, because haunts of
violence fill the dark places of the land. 21 Do not let the oppressed retreat in disgrace; may the
poor and needy praise your name. 22 Rise up, O God, and defend your cause; remember how
fools mock you all day long. 23 Do not ignore the clamor of your adversaries, the uproar of your
enemies, which rises continually.

ANALYSIS QUESTIONS

1. Why might a thinker focused only on deductive reasoning have difficulty understanding and explaining this text?
2. What does this author presume about the power of God in the first 11 verses?
3. Why do you think the writer feels he needs to remind God of his mighty works in verses 12-17?
4. In verses 18-23 the author presumes to tell the Almighty precisely how to run the world. How have the first 17 verses prepared the reader for the argument that concludes the passage?
5. One eternal philosophical question about God asks, "If God is all powerful, why is there evil in the world?" Another asks, "Why do the evil prosper while good people suffer?" In what ways does Asaph approach these issues? How successful is he?

6. What have you learned from this passage about inductive reasoning that will be useful in writing your own argument?

Jeremiah 12: Inductive Argument Using Rhetorical Questions

[1] You are always righteous, O LORD, when I bring a case before you. Yet I would speak with you about your justice: Why does the way of the wicked prosper? Why do all the faithless live at ease? [2] You have planted them, and they have taken root; they grow and bear fruit. You are always on their lips but far from their hearts. [3] Yet you know me, O LORD; you see me and test my thoughts about you. Drag them off like sheep to be butchered! Set them apart for the day of slaughter! [4] How long will the land lie parched and the grass in every field be withered? Because those who live in it are wicked, the animals and birds have perished. Moreover, the people are saying, "He will not see what happens to us."

God's Answer

[5] "If you have raced with men on foot and they have worn you out, how can you compete with horses? If you stumble in safe country, how will you manage in the thickets by the Jordan? [6] Your brothers, your own family—even they have betrayed you; they have raised a loud cry against you. Do not trust them, though they speak well of you.

[7] "I will forsake my house, abandon my inheritance; I will give the one I love into the hands of her enemies. [8] My inheritance has become to me like a lion in the forest. She roars at me; therefore I hate her. [9] Has not my inheritance become to me like a speckled bird of prey that other birds of prey surround and attack? Go and gather all the wild beasts; bring them to devour.

[10] Many shepherds will ruin my vineyard and trample down my field; they will turn my pleasant field into a desolate wasteland. [11] It will be made a wasteland, parched and desolate before me; the whole land will be laid waste because there is no one who cares. [12] Over all the barren heights in the desert destroyers will swarm, for the sword of the LORD will devour from

one end of the land to the other; no one will be safe. [13] They will sow wheat but reap thorns; they
will wear themselves out but gain nothing. So bear the shame of your harvest because of the
LORD's fierce anger."

[14] This is what the LORD says: "As for all my wicked neighbors who seize the
inheritance I gave my people Israel, I will uproot them from their lands and I will uproot the
house of Judah from among them. [15] But after I uproot them, I will again have compassion and
will bring each of them back to his own inheritance and his own country. [16] And if they learn
well the ways of my people and swear by my name, saying, 'As surely as the LORD lives'-even
as they once taught my people to swear by Baal—then they will be established among my
people. [17] But if any nation does not listen, I will completely uproot and destroy it," declares the
LORD.

ANALYSIS QUESTIONS

7. Put Jeremiah's complaint in verses 1-4 into your own words.
8. Put God's counter-complaint in verses 5-13 into your own words.
9. What about God's long-range perspective in verses 14-17 might comfort Jeremiah?

THE NATURE OF GREAT SPEAKING: I HAVE A DREAM

Michael Osborn argues convincingly that "I Have a Dream" is one of the greatest speeches in history. This claim challenges the notion that deductive logic is essential for successful argument. To assess whether his claims are true, first read King's speech, which follows.

I Have a Dream

I am happy to join with you today in what will go down in history as the greatest demonstration for freedom in the history of our nation.

Five score years ago, a great American, in whose symbolic shadow we stand today, signed the Emancipation Proclamation. This momentous decree came as a great beacon light of hope to millions of Negro slaves who had been seared in the flames of withering injustice. It came as a joyous daybreak to end the long night of their captivity.

But one hundred years later, the Negro still is not free. One hundred years later, the life of the Negro is still sadly crippled by the manacles of segregation and the chains of discrimination. One hundred years later, the Negro lives on a lonely island of poverty in the midst of a vast ocean of material prosperity. One hundred years later, the Negro is still languishing in the corners of American society and finds himself an exile in his own land. So we have come here today to dramatize a shameful condition.

In a sense we have come to our nation's capital to cash a check. When the architects of our republic wrote the magnificent words of the Constitution and the Declaration of Independence, they were signing a promissory note to which every American was to fall heir. This note was a promise that all men, yes, black men as well as white men, would be guaranteed the unalienable rights of life, liberty, and the pursuit of happiness.

It is obvious today that America has defaulted on this promissory note insofar as her citizens of color are concerned. Instead of honoring this sacred obligation, America has given the Negro people a bad check, a check which has come back marked "insufficient funds." But we refuse to believe that the bank of justice is bankrupt. We refuse to believe that there are insufficient funds in the great vaults of opportunity of this nation. So we have come to cash this check—a check that will give us upon demand the riches of freedom and the security of justice. We have also come to this hallowed spot to remind America of the fierce urgency of now. This is no time to engage in the luxury of cooling off or to take the tranquilizing drug of gradualism. Now is the time to make real the promises of democracy. Now is the time to rise from the dark and desolate valley of segregation to the sunlit path of racial justice. Now is the time to lift our nation from the quick sands of racial injustice to the solid rock of brotherhood. Now is the time to make justice a reality for all of God's children.

It would be fatal for the nation to overlook the urgency of the moment. This sweltering summer of the Negro's legitimate discontent will not pass until there is an invigorating autumn of freedom and equality. Nineteen sixty-three is not an end, but a beginning. Those who hope that the Negro needed to blow off steam and will now be content will have a rude awakening if the nation returns to business as usual. There will be neither rest nor tranquility in America until the Negro is granted his citizenship rights. The whirlwinds of revolt will continue to shake the foundations of our nation until the bright day of justice emerges.

But there is something that I must say to my people who stand on the warm threshold which leads into the palace of justice. In the process of gaining our rightful place we must not be guilty of wrongful deeds. Let us not seek to satisfy our thirst for freedom by drinking from the cup of bitterness and hatred.

We must forever conduct our struggle on the high plane of dignity and discipline. We must not allow our creative protest to degenerate into physical violence. Again and again we must rise to the majestic heights of meeting physical force with soul force. The marvelous new militancy which has engulfed the Negro community must not lead us to a distrust of all white people, for many of our white brothers, as evidenced by their presence here today, have come to realize that their destiny is tied up with our destiny and their freedom is inextricably bound to our freedom. We cannot walk alone.

As we walk, we must make the pledge that we shall always march ahead. We cannot turn back. There are those who are asking the devotees of civil rights, "When will you be satisfied?" We can never be satisfied as long as the Negro is the victim of the unspeakable horrors of police brutality. We can never be satisfied, as long as our bodies, heavy with the fatigue of travel, cannot gain lodging in the motels of the highways and the hotels of the cities. We cannot be satisfied as long as the Negro's basic mobility is from a smaller ghetto to a larger one.We can never be satisfied as long as a Negro in Mississippi cannot vote and a Negro in New York believes he has nothing for which to vote. No, no, we are not satisfied, and we will not be satisfied until justice rolls down like waters and righteousness like a mighty stream.

I am not unmindful that some of you have come here out of great trials and tribulations. Some of you have come fresh from narrow jail cells. Some of you have come from areas where your quest for freedom left you battered by the storms of persecution and staggered by the winds of police brutality. You have been the veterans of creative suffering. Continue to work with the faith that unearned suffering is redemptive.

Go back to Mississippi, go back to Alabama, go back to South Carolina, go back to Georgia, go back to Louisiana, go back to the slums and ghettos of our northern cities, knowing that somehow this situation can and will be changed. Let us not wallow in the valley of despair.

I say to you today, my friends, that in spite of the difficulties and frustrations of the moment,[2] I still have a dream. It is a dream deeply rooted in the American dream.

I have a dream that one day this nation will rise up and live out the true meaning of its creed: "We hold these truths to be self-evident: that all men are created equal."

I have a dream that one day on the red hills of Georgia the sons of former slaves and the sons of former slave owners will be able to sit down together at the table of brotherhood.

I have a dream that one day even the state of Mississippi, a state sweltering with the heat of injustice, sweltering with the heat of oppression, will be transformed into an oasis of freedom and justice.

I have a dream that my four little children will one day live in a nation where they will not be judged by the color of their skin but by the content of their character.

I have a dream today.

I have a dream that one day, down in Alabama, with its vicious racists, with its governor having his lips dripping with the words of interposition and nullification; one day right there in Alabama, little black boys and black girls will be able to join hands with little white boys and white girls as sisters and brothers.

I have a dream today.

I have a dream that one day every valley shall be exalted, every hill and mountain shall be made low, the rough places will be made plain, and the crooked places will be made straight, and the glory of the Lord shall be revealed, and all flesh shall see it together.

This is our hope. This is the faith that I go back to the South with. With this faith we will be able to hew out of the mountain of despair a stone of hope. With this faith we will be able to transform the jangling discords of our nation into a beautiful symphony of brotherhood. With this faith we will be able to work together, to pray together, to struggle together, to go to jail together, to stand up for freedom together, knowing that we will be free one day.

---

[2] King's spoken address differs from his prepared script. The spoken address reads, "so even though we face the difficulties of today and tomorrow…."

This will be the day when all of God's children will be able to sing with a new meaning, "My country, 'tis of thee, sweet land of liberty, of thee I sing. Land where my fathers died, land of the pilgrim's pride, from every mountainside, let freedom ring."

And if America is to be a great nation this must become true. So let freedom ring from the prodigious hilltops of New Hampshire. Let freedom ring from the mighty mountains of New York. Let freedom ring from the heightening Alleghenies of Pennsylvania!

Let freedom ring from the snowcapped Rockies of Colorado!

Let freedom ring from the curvaceous slopes of California!

But not only that; let freedom ring from Stone Mountain of Georgia!

Let freedom ring from Lookout Mountain of Tennessee!

Let freedom ring from every hill and molehill of Mississippi. From every mountainside, let freedom ring.

And when this happens, When we allow freedom to ring, when we let it ring from every village and every hamlet, from every state and every city, we will be able to speed up that day when all of God's children, black men and white men, Jews and Gentiles, Protestants and Catholics, will be able to join hands and sing in the words of the old Negro spiritual, "Free at last! free at last! thank God Almighty, we are free at last!"

WHY IT'S GREAT

Below are Michael Osborn's reasons for believing that "I Have a Dream" is one of the greatest speeches in history (Osborn). Two thousand years ago the Roman Longinus wrote *On the Sublime*, a study in great public speaking. "Sublimity is the echo of a great soul," says Longinus. Great speeches accomplish the following:

1. Elevate the Mind: If the speech is to be great, there must be greatness in the speaker. Aristotle observed that an audience will accept a speaker's message if the points are adequately

proved. He said we have a divine spark in our nature that makes us receptive to greatness, and he captures this greatness with three words: *Ethos* (trust), *Pathos* (emotional appeal), and *Logos* (reason) are all necessary for greatness. When your critics are also won over, it is truly a great speech. King accomplishes this by calling on the constitution, associating himself with Lincoln and the Gettysburg address, and the hymn "Let Freedom Ring." By associating his movement with the vital symbols of American life, he put those who opposed him on the defensive and himself in the mainstream.

2. <u>Have Superior Structure</u>: The way material is organized, building to a dramatic climax, is vital. The broken American promise is spoken of in the shadow of the Lincoln Memorial. King uses four movements in the speech: 1. He expresses historical perspective and cultural outrage; 2. He exposes the nature of the injustice—we can never be satisfied *until*.... This allows him to set up his agenda for social change; 3. He shares his dream—his vision of a better life. He moves from being an advocate to becoming a prophet who sees the future in all the fullness of its meaning; 4. He says, "Let freedom ring"—he wills his vision to be fulfilled and declares, "I've seen the promised land."

3. <u>Use Bold Imagery</u>: This passes the bounds of mere persuasion. With startling images we are drawn away from mere logic and brilliance. King makes us *see* his message. In his use of imagery, King is in the top five spokespersons in the history of western culture along with Demosthenes, finest of the ancient Greek world; Cicero, finest of the classical Roman orators; Edmond Burke, best of the British in the age of eloquence; and Abraham Lincoln, powerful American orator who used simple images with profound meanings.

4. <u>Present a Great Challenge</u>: Osborn adds to the Longinus criteria that some great cultural crisis must call forth greatness in the speaker to rise to the nobility of the moment.

What circumstance did King face? ______________________________________

What circumstance do you face? ____

No doubt that pressing concern will become the topic of your argument.

5. Offer Transport: The effect of elevated language is not persuasion, but transport—sublimity flashing forth at the right moment … displaying the power of the orator in all of its fullness. It is almost like being born anew. The audience is given new eyes to see through. The meaning of their lives looks and feels different. King himself was forever different after this speech. He was transported into being a representative for freedom—he received the Nobel Peace Prize.

Osborn says great speeches offer depiction, emotion, and identification. They also incite to action, and they commemorate the past. Inductive argument is often superior to deductive argument for the same reasons. Longinus: "That is truly great which bears repeated examination, in which it is difficult or even impossible to withstand, and the memory of which is strong and hard to efface" (Osborn).

BONUS SECTION: INTEGRATION

The first section of this text taught the writing techniques of narrative, description, process, definition, illustration, and classification. The second section taught how to write comparison and media analysis essays. The third section taught the fundamentals of cause and effect, deductive, and inductive arguments. This final section suggests that students write an integration paper by selecting material from all (or most) of the previous papers and combine them into one fully developed argument in the student's chosen field of study. Such integration requires three-dimensional writing that draws on all the writing styles taught in this text.

INTEGRATION MODEL

The book of Hebrews is a masterful integration paper drawing on more than 80 Old Testament passages to demonstrate in a powerful argument that the earlier covenant between God and humanity is fulfilled in Jesus Christ. The author uses all the knowledge of Jewish scripture and tradition as well as every tool of communication and persuasion available to him in this demonstration that both Hebrew and Gentile believers can and should be integrated into the one Church.

WRITING ASSIGNMENT

The first step is to establish an outline for the integration paper. This outline should be an expanded version of the structure recommended in the argument writing assignment from Chapter 10. Once the outline is established, it is relatively easy to cut and paste the material from previous papers into one document organized in such a way that it anticipates the reader's questions and answers them in a logical and satisfying manner. Once the basic structure is in place, the writer must tie the manuscript together with excellent transitions.

Transitions are words and phrases that serve as bridges from one paragraph to the next, one section to the next, and one chapter to the next. Transitions guide readers and prevent them from getting lost in the reading. Transitions serve as glue to hold an essay together.

Avoid over-using transitions. They are not needed between every sentence, but they are often needed between each paragraph. In a longer work, transition sentences and sometimes entire paragraphs are needed to guide the reader's thinking from what has been said so far to what will be explained next. Many kinds of transitions are possible, and a variety of examples are provided below.[1]

Transitions to emphasize a point:

Again	another key point	first thing to remember
For this reason	frequently	important to realize
Indeed	in fact	to repeat
Most compelling evidence	most important information	must be remembered
On the negative side	on the positive side	point often overlooked
Significant that	surprisingly	truly
To emphasize	to point out	with this in mind

Transitions to show location:

Above	across	against	along	alongside	amid
Among	around	away from	back of	behind	below
Beneath	beside	between	beyond	by	down
Into	near	off	on top of	outside	over

[1] Charts condensed from *Kim's Korner for Teacher Talk.*

Throughout	under	on	inside	in front of	in the center of
in the middle of		to the left	to the right		

Transitions to compare items:

As	also	accordingly	comparable to
Like	likewise	similarly	sometimes
Just as	in the same way		in conjunction with this

Transitions to contrast items:

Although	as opposed to	but	conversely	counter to
Even so	even though	however	in spite of	in the meantime
Otherwise	sometimes	still	yet	
Nevertheless	on the contrary		on the other hand	

Transitions to show time:

About	after	afterward	as soon as	at	at the same time
Before	during	finally	first	later	in the meantime
Meanwhile	meanwhile	last	next week	next time	next year
Immediately	prior to	soon	yesterday	today	Tomorrow
Until	when	then	next		

Transitions to clarify:

For example	for instance	to illustrate	put another way
To clarify	simply stated	that is	stated differently

Transitions to add information:

Additionally	again	along with	also	and	another
As well	besides	equally important		finally	for example

For instance	further	furthermore	in addition	likewise	moreover
Next	together with				

Transitions to conclude or summarize:

Accordingly	as a result	consequently	due to	finally	in closing
In short	in summary	therefore	thus	lastly	in the last analysis
Logical conclusion is					

Transitions to enumerate (to be used as sets):

First	second	third
One important	equally important	most important
A significant	another significant	of greatest significance
First	next	last
In the beginning	toward the middle	at the end
One	also	in addition

HEART OF DARKNESS

In addition to words and phrases, writers also use sentence and paragraph transitions to move the reader to the next phase of the presentation. A classic example is provided by Joseph Conrad in *Heart of Darkness* where for dozens of pages the reader has been on a riverboat exploring the African interior. On the return journey the narrator becomes extremely ill, and the reader is efficiently transported back to civilization:

> No, they did not bury me, though there is a period of time which I remember mistily, with a shuddering wonder, like a passage through some inconceivable world that had no hope in it and no desire. I found myself back in the sepulchral city resenting the sight of people hurrying through the streets to

> filch a little money from each other, to devour their infamous cookery, to gulp their unwholesome beer, to dream their insignificant and silly dreams. (90)

In just eight words, "I found myself back in the sepulchral city," Conrad transports the narrative to another continent while showing the reader that darkness is as pervasive in Europe as it is in Africa. Writers employ this transition technique whenever cumbersome and unnecessary details get in the way.

THE HONORS THESIS

The integration paper based on all the assignments in this book is likely to grow into a long manuscript—possibly as much as 35 pages. And if all the sources researched are included, the Works Cited may easily be two or three pages in length. Writing such a paper prepares students for the honors thesis that they may have the opportunity to write toward the end of their undergraduate program in college. At the very least, the integration paper will demonstrate the comprehensive knowledge gained throughout the semester, and reveal to the students that they have not only honed their writing and research skills, they have also attained a meaningful education within their chosen discipline and learned to effectively communicate what they know.

WORKS CITED

"Alexander Borodin: Biography." *Classic Cat.* Web. 17 Apr. 2009.

"Alexander Graham Bell: Inventor." *Lucid Café.* (29 Feb. 2008): n. pag. Web. 21 Apr. 2009.

Augustin. *City of God. Nicene and Post-Nicene Fathers,* vol. 2. Ed. Philip Schaff, 14 vols. Peabody, MA: Hendrickson, 2004. Print.

"APA Formatting and Style Guide." *The Owl at Perdue.* Web. 4 Apr. 2009.

Anthanasius the Great. *The Life of St. Anthony the Great.* Willits, CA: Eastern Orthodox Books, n.d. Date of original publication AD 357. Print.

Bach, Johann Sebastian. *Fugue in G Minor. Edition Bacakademie*. Dir. Helmuth Rilling, perf. Kay Johannsen, Organ Stiftschurch Grauhof. Holzgerlingen, Germany, 1999. CD.

Bates, Gerald E. "A Taste of African Imagination." *World Mission People: The Best of* The Missionary Tidings*, 1990-95.* Ed. Daniel V. Runyon. Spring Arbor, MI: Saltbox Press, 1995: 146-147. Print.

The Bible. New International Version. Ed. Kenneth Barker. Grand Rapids: Zondervan, 2000. Print. Other editions cited in text where quoted.

Bulwer-Lytton, Edward George. *Pelham: Or The Adventures of a Gentleman.* Lincoln: U of Nebraska P, 1972. Print.

Bunyan, John. *The Holy War.* Eds. Roger Sharrock and James Forrest. Oxford: Clarendon, 1980. Print.

Carr, Karen. "Socrates." *Kidipede—History for Kids.* Web. 17 Apr. 2009.

Chesterton, G. K. "A Defence of Slang." *The Defendant.* London: J. M. Dent & Sons, 1901. Print.

Conrad, Joseph. *Heart of Darkness.* New York: Airmont, 1966. Print.

Dalton, Joan. "Applying Bloom's Taxonomy." *Good Questions are the Key to Good Research* (1986): n. pag. Web. 9 Apr. 2009.

Dillard, Annie. *Teaching a Stone to Talk: Expeditions and Encounters.* New York: Harper & Row, 1982. Print.

Ellison, Ralph. *Invisible Man.* New York: Random House, 1980. Print.

Elmer, Duane. *Cross-Cultural Connections.* Downers Grove, IL: IVP Academic, 2002. Print.

Frye, Northrop. *Anatomy of Criticism.* Princeton: Princeton UP, 1957. Print.

---. *The Great Code: The Bible and Literature.* New York: Harcourt Brace Jovanovich, 1982. Print.

Gaebelein, Frank E., ed. *The Expositor's Bible Commentary.* 12 vols. Grand Rapids: Zondervan, 1976. Print.

Goodpaster, Jeffery R. *Thinking.* Upper Saddle River, NJ: Prentice Hall, 1999. Print.

Hemingway, Ernest. *For Whom the Bell Tolls.* New York: Charles Scribner's Sons, 1940. Print.

Henn, T. R. *The Bible as Literature.* New York: Oxford UP, 1970. Print.

Ishii, Satoshi. "Thought Patterns as Modes of Rhetoric: The United States and Japan." *Intercultural Communication: A Reader*. Eds. Larry A. Samovar and Richard E. Porter. 4th ed. Belmont, CA: Wadsworth, 1985: 97-102. Print.

Jefferson, Thomas. Letter to Richard Price. 8 Jan. 1789. The Thomas Jefferson Papers, Manuscript Division of the Library of Congress. Web. 7 May 2009.

Kim's Korner for Teacher Talk. Ed. Kimberly Steele. Web. 22 May 2009.

King, Jr., Martin Luther. "I Have a Dream." Lincoln Memorial, Washington D.C. 28 Aug. 1963.

Web. 25 May 2009. <http://www.mlkonline.net/dream.html>.

Lewis, C. S. *Letters to Malcolm: Chiefly on Prayer.* New York: Harcourt, Brace & World, 1964.

---. *The Four Loves*. Oxford: Clarendon, 1967. Print.

Lincoln, Abraham. Second Inaugural Address. March 4, 1865. Yale Law School: The Avalon Project. 25 Oct. 2005. Web. 7 Apr. 2009.

Lynch, Beth. "'Rather Dark to Readers in General': Some Critical Casualties of John Bunyan's *Holy War* (1682)." *Bunyan Studies* 9 (1999/2000): 25-49. Print.

MLA Handbook for Writers of Research Papers: Seventh Edition. New York: The Modern Language Association of America, 2009. Print.

Newton, Isaac. "A Letter of Mr. Isaac Newton," *The Norton Anthology of English Literature*, 8th ed. Vol. 1. Ed. Stephen Greenblatt. New York: W. W. Norton, 2006: 2156-2160. Print.

Osborn, Michael. *I Have a Dream: The Nature of Great Speaking.* Davidson Films, n.d. Film.

Pushkin, Alexander. "The Queen of Spades." *Great Russian Short Stories*. New York: Bantam Dobleday Dell, 1958. Print.

Runyon, Kirby. Message to the author. 22 Sept. 2005. E-mail.

Ryken, Leland. "Literary Criticism of the Bible: Some Fallacies." *Literary Interpretations of Biblical Narratives.* Ed. Kenneth R. R. Gros Louis. Nashville: Abingdon, 1974. Print.

---. *The Literature of the Bible.* Grand Rapids: Zondervan, 1974. Print.

"Sterile." *Shorter Oxford English Dictionary.* 5th ed. 2002. Print.

Snyder, Howard A., with Daniel V. Runyon. *Decoding the Church: Mapping the DNA of Christ's Body.* Grand Rapids: Baker, 2002. Print.

Strunk, William, Jr., and E. B. White. *The Elements of Style.* Needham Heights, MA: Allen & Bacon, 2000. Print.

Truss, Lynne. *Eats, Shoots & Leaves*. New York: Gotham Books, 2003. Print.

Twain, Mark. *The Innocents Abroad; or, The New Pilgrims' Progress.* Vol. 2. New York: Harper & Brothers, 1911. First published in 1869 by the American Publishing Company. Print.

---. "Continued Perplexities." *Life on the Mississippi.* London: Oxford UP, 1962. Print.

---. *Life on the Mississippi.* London: Oxford UP, 1973. Print.

Van Biema, David. "Why We Should Teach the Bible in Public School." *Time* 2 Apr. 2007: 40-46. Print.

Wellek, Rene and Austin Warren. "The Nature of Literature." *Theory of Literature*. 3rd ed. New York: Harcourt, Brace and World, 1956. Print.

White, Charles. "The Puzzle of Systematic Theology." Unpublished essay, 2006. Print.

"The Wright Story." *First-to-Fly.* (28 Aug. 2006): n. pag. Web. 17 Apr. 2009.